I0202014

GOD'S
BUSINESS

http://www.gods-business.com

GOD'S
BUSINESS

Making Church Leaders

<u>Less Stressed</u> and

<u>More Effective</u> by Leveraging

The Experience of Others

Kurt M. Glacy, MBA, MDiv, MSM

http://www.gods-business.com

Copyright @ 2015 by Kurt M. Glacy, MBA, MDiv, MSM

Published by LEVR Consulting, LLC., Spring Hill, Florida

All rights reserved. No part of this book may be reproduced, stored or transmitted by any means – whether auditory, graphic, mechanical, or electronic – without written permission of both publisher and author, except in the case of brief excerpts used in critical articles and reviews. Unauthorized reproduction of any part of this work is illegal and punishable by law.

Because of the dynamic nature of the Internet, any web addresses or links contained in this book may have changed since publication and may no longer be valid.

Paperback ISBN: 978-0692637463

eBook ISBN: 978-0692699201

Disclaimer

The experiences and recommendations contained in this book may not be relevant to every congregation, pastor, or church leader. The author's intent is to present his observations about strengths and failings in different churches over the course of more than three decades. It is also the intent to share some experiences and best practices from other clergy and church leaders from various denominations and regions across the United States.

The author obtained information found in this book from sources that he considered to be reliable, including direct experience, personal conversations, online surveys, and group round-table discussions. The author does not intend or imply to guarantee accuracy. The author is not in the business of giving legal, accounting, or other specialized business advice. Should readers need such advice, he or she should engage with specific subject matter experts directly.

The author disclaims any liability, loss, or risk taken by individuals and congregations who directly or indirectly act on the information provided by this book, or that is contained on the associated website: www.gods-business.com. The author strongly believes that the experiences and recommendations found in the book are reliable. However, he cannot be held responsible for readers' actions or their results.

Contributors

This book would not have been possible without the active participation of the following people:

Rev. Glenn Mortimer, MDiv – Pastor, Wakefield/Lynnfield United Methodist Church, Wakefield, Massachusetts

Cathy Meyer, MSM - Minister of Music and Organist, Memorial Congregational Church, Sudbury, Massachusetts

Rev. Victoria Alford Guest, MDiv, MTS – Pastor, First Congregational Church, Natick, Massachusetts

Rev. Nathan Robinson, MDiv - Pastor, Emmanuel Lutheran Church, Woodstock, Virginia

Terry Lagree - Senior Warden, St. Anne's Episcopal Church, Crystal River, Florida; President, Barbaron, Inc. and Founder of Harmony Links Golf

Rev. Ned Allyn Parker, MDiv – Pastor for Children, Families and Young Adults, Seattle First Baptist Church, Seattle, Washington

Rev. Robert Asinger, MDiv – Senior Minister, Church by the Sea, Bal Harbour, Florida

Rev. Kari Nicewander, MDiv –Pastor, Immanuel Congregational Church, Hartford, Connecticut and former Discipleship and Church Growth Specialist for The Church of Central Africa Presbyterian, Synod of Zambia

Keith Blackman, CPA, CMA, CGMA, CM&AA – Principal, Nperspective CFO & Strategic Services, Tampa, Florida

Zeke Mathena – Co-Founder, Tactical Defense Training Center, Crystal River, Florida

Ronni Marshak, Executive Vice President – Patricia Seybold Group, Boston, Massachusetts

Elizabeth "Betty" Norlin - Author and Entrepreneur, Tampa, Florida

Tasha Vincent, MBA, Software Product Manager – Pearson Education, Boston, Massachusetts

Table of Contents

Foreword

Kurt Glacy and I met in seminary at Boston University in 2003. We became instant friends as we both had similar backgrounds. Kurt had run his own business and was a musician, and I had spent the first 20 years of my working life as a violinist and an arts administrator, ending my administrative career as the manager of ensembles for the School of Music at Yale University.

What surprised me most when Kurt and I were in seminary was the lack of real-world knowledge and experience that was provided to these folks who were going to be going out and leading a local church. Didn't the seminary know that the pastor had to know more than know how to preach on Sunday, visit the sick, and bury the dead? They also had to know how to talk to the building inspector and fix the leaky faucet and where the fuse box was. I suppose that I was fortunate in knowing what to expect as my father was a pastor, and I watched as he had to be jack-of-all-trades when it came to not just leading the church, but running the church.

When Kurt approached me and others with the idea of putting a book together that would help future generations of pastors and lay people understand that a key element of the work of the church was missing, I

12

knew that God had a hand in this book coming to life. The element that the church was missing was that the church must exist as a business in order to continue to be a church.

Many people believe that the "church" is different. We cannot use the word "business" in the same sentence as the word "church"; somehow it seems sacrilegious. If we examine the church in our culture and society today, you would probably see many similarities to a business. No, the church does not sell anything or manufacture a product, but it does provide a service. The business the church is in is God's business, and, in order to do God's business in the world, the church must run like any other business. My friend and colleague Kurt Glacy gives us that insight and spiritual thoughtfulness to go beyond the liturgy and the stained glass windows. Kurt moves us out of the organ loft and the choir stalls to the place where the nitty gritty of the church meets the world.

As a pastor, I must profess that they teach us a lot about theological reflection, biblical studies, and all kinds of academic prowess; however, that isn't going to help you develop a budget for a struggling church; it isn't going to help you figure out how to manage the physical plant of your edifice; and it certainly isn't going to help you talk to your trustees and staff about the issues that befall the church of the 21st Century. Kurt takes all of this, and more, into account as he brings to light the resources, skills, and knowledge that every pastor must have to run their parish in this changing and challenging world. Contained in *God's Business* are the resources you didn't get when you went to seminary, along with the truth about how you really do need to know something about business in order to run a vibrant and spiritually driven church.

Kurt takes his years of business experience and his faith, along with his vast network of friends who work in the church, to weave a text that will become the business bible of how pastors can run their church successfully and navigate the core business aspects of the church, so that we can reach out to help a needy world. I commend to you the pages before you as a journey to help God fulfill his work in the world through you as you go about doing "God's Business".

Rev. Glenn M. Mortimer, M.Div. Pastor
Wakefield/Lynnfield United Methodist Church
Wakefield, Massachusetts

Chapter 1: Purpose of the Book

Congratulations! The mere fact that you picked up this book indicates that you have a desire to make your ministry and your church thrive. With the current reality being that a vast number of mainline churches are in a state of decline in attendance and influence, the role of pastor and church leader has become more important than ever.

According to informal polls taken over the years (in person and online), it is readily acknowledged that seminaries make little or no effort to provide real-world, proven instruction on how to make an organization be successful. In most cases, recent seminary graduates are placed into positions where the church is really struggling in almost every aspect of its existence.

While seminaries do a wonderful job preparing men and women to serve their communities in terms of pastoral care, worship and liturgy, and faith formation, historically, these institutions have not adequately prepared pastors of small churches for the day-to-day operations and management of the church. The stress caused by this lack of experience can have a negative impact on the lives and ministries of church leaders.

This book can help provide insights and, hopefully, some encouragement to you, so that you can navigate these non-pastoral issues effectively and keep your valuable time and energy focused on the really important things.

Let's be clear about something, though. Most of us hopefully believe that the mission of church is not to make a lot of money and to have a lot of property. Those metrics may make sense for large, publicly-held businesses. For God's Business, however, the things that we need to be working toward include transforming lives through the sacraments, through education, through prayer, through engagement in and out of worship, and through meaningful, grace-filled relationships.

If you work for a "rich" church but do not have these things, then you are already bankrupt! However, if you have all of these things but cannot afford to keep your ministry going, then you are also bankrupt! Our churches, regardless of their denomination and model (street ministry, house church, or a church with a physical location), need to operate in the middle of the road. That is to say that the church needs to be run with God's objectives in mind, not our own. And our churches also have to run effectively and wisely in order to keep the resources that we need to operate flowing freely.

Biblical Reasoning

Many in our profession will argue that the church is not a business and therefore should not be run like one. This may be true depending on how you define what a business is. However, there is no denying that with no money, we cannot carry out our mission. Also, treating our volunteers, employees, and members in a way that any other customer or employee would want to be treated is not only Biblically sound, but practical as well. Perhaps we will do better to view our churches and ministries as a sort of franchise from God, where we acknowledge that everything that we do, from the ministerial to the managerial, portrays God either positively or negatively to the world.

Examining the parables of Jesus in Matthew 24 and 25, we hear clear expectations of the master/worker relationship. In our churches and ministries, it is imperative that we remember that God is the master, not us. Therefore, we are accountable to God in all aspects of the church, including management and leadership.

Personal Reasoning

People rarely become pastors or church leaders so that they can deal with teams that may be somewhat dysfunctional, oversee financial resources (or the lack thereof), and deal with buildings and systems that are in need of repair. The reality is, however, that, at some point, most of us will encounter these daunting issues and many more. What usually motivates all of us is having the opportunity to serve our congregations and communities in pastoral ways through counselling services, leading worship, pastoral care visits, and faith-formation activities.

This book provides you with a quick go-to resource that will highlight some issues that other congregations have faced, and some useful tools and insights so that you can navigate these issues effectively if and when they come up in your ministry. Each chapter may not be relevant to you at any given time. However, when issues or questions crop up in your church, you can get a quick idea of how similar situations have (or have not) been handled in other places.

The real value of this book is that other successful pastors and church leaders, just like you, share their experience and wisdom with us so that we can effectively handle difficult situations, seamlessly lead our congregations in both faith and function, and devote the maximum amount of time on what is really important – God's Business.

Business Reasoning

Most congregations today are not thriving. Like a small business, when people end their relationship with us and new ones no longer respond to what we offer, then it is time to reevaluate and make a pivot. This book is not intended to tell you how to make a change in your vision or mission. What it does do is help you identify when you may need to make that pivot, and how to successfully lead a team of paid staff and volunteers to achieve success in the new paradigm.

Chances are that our congregations need a little help in regaining their focus on what is really important. When churches begin to enter a state of decline, the focus becomes increasingly inward, and conflicts arise around membership levels and revenue and the seemingly insurmountable task of making ends meet while attracting new people into our worship services. In order to regain our outward vision and create and implement a strategy to accomplish it, effective management is required so that church operations and structure do not interfere with growth strategies and activities.

Some pastors and church leaders come to the table with significant experience in managing for-profit and non-profit industries. Even those that are blessed with this type of background still need to occasionally brush up on some of their operational skills. So, unless you already have a highly successful team, meet all of the church's goals, and you have a crystal clear vision of where you are going with your ministry, then this book is for you.

Book Layout

The chapters in this book are in order, starting with the most basic needs for a church plant (or a church rescue). From there, chapters become more granular toward specific operations and procedures that come into place as organizations grow in congregational size and tangible assets. Some chapters may be of little or no use to you unless your ministry already has other key components in place; and none of them alone can create a successful ministry. They are only details that must be considered to keep an organization running smoothly so that strategic vision and growth can take place.

If you find yourself needing a little more help in any area, please feel free to contact us. We are here to help you be the very best pastor and church leader that we know you can be.

Chapter 2: Marketing: Vision and Strategy

Chapter Overview

In terms of this book, marketing is about the strategy of an organization, and leadership is about how to get this to happen. Marketing is not about promotion and evangelism. It is not about how we get more people in our church. Marketing is an outside-in activity, not an inside-out activity. Marketing is how we get our church out into the community and how we can address the needs of the people that we find there. Only when we have completed a marketing assessment for a community and a plan of action can we then develop small groups, targeted ministries, and other programs that are truly useful. These programs themselves are part of our ministries and operations, yet, to understand the true heart of the process, they are the result of marketing activities, not the marketing itself.

There is a concept that marketing means advertising and sales. For the purpose of this book, marketing is not sales, advertising, or promotion. Marketing is the process where we determine how we are going to act as a community. Think of it as a business strategy. In business, you do a gap analysis where you look at the needs of your community, and then you build your organization, product or business around that. The analysis and competitive landscape include: What are the other types of businesses, religious organizations, and spiritual organizations that are already in the area? What needs are they currently serving? What needs are not being met? We want to consider how we can organize to meet the needs of our community: Will we be a free-standing church, a street ministry, or a digital ministry? What is our outreach plan? Who are we people that we are going to serve? What services and resources are we going to provide? Where are we going to provide it?

Who

Determining whom to serve will largely depend on the vision and passion of the church leader or pastor. We are all given certain gifts and burdens on our hearts that will make us more effective when we follow them. We can also verify the needs from that pastor by looking at the area and doing a focused analysis. How is the community currently being served? For example, if we have a desire to create a new ministry for people who are unchurched, we would need to look at how many people in our target population are currently unchurched, why they are unchurched, and what their belief systems may be already (many people unaffiliated with a church are neither agnostic nor atheistic, by the way!). What are the issues that they deal with on a daily basis, and what are their celebrations? What do they think most about, and how can our ministry address those things?

It is important for us as pastors and church leaders to be aware and willing to accept that the people we are trying to attract will change us as much as we are attempting to change them. Radical hospitality goes in both directions. When we invite people into our churches for worship and fellowship, their backgrounds, beliefs, and customs will influence us in the same way that ours will influence them. Without a willingness to grow and embrace the change that will result from welcoming new people, it will be impossible for our ministry to flourish.

Having had ministerial roles in many different types of churches over the last thirty-plus years, I have seen many pastors with the heart to grow their churches. However, when new people come with new ideas and their own traditions, there is often an institutional resistance to actually welcoming change. For example, if you say that you welcome all kinds of people and that you want everyone to have a voice, yet you are unwilling to listen, the pursuit of lasting growth is useless.

At our seminary, most faculty and students prided themselves of their self-perception of radical hospitality. Staying on the forefront of social movements and making bold statements about welcoming everyone was a goal that was clearly stated and widely understood. However, there were problems for students who had views and beliefs that were considered to be "too conservative." These students appeared to be excluded in some conversations and targeted in others. Because they were not deemed to be welcoming, they themselves were not welcomed by the "liberal" students. Why couldn't our "welcoming" colleagues see the log in their own eye?

What

The "what" in congregational marketing relates to the type of ministry we are considering holding. In most cases, Americans think about a Sunday morning service where we sit in pews and listen to a sermon. Maybe we meet sometimes during the week as well. Others may have more informal gathering places, like a coffee house, pub, or a residence where we can worship and have conversations. Finally, others may gather in huge arenas.

24

Worship may take place during the day or the evening, and not always on a Sunday.

When we consider the people we are trying to serve in a new or revised ministry, we want to look at their schedules. For example, when single moms want to worship with us, they may already have to work on Sunday mornings to earn a living for their families. Sunday mornings may not work for them; so will we provide times when they can come either with or without their children? If they come with their children, will we have youth programs that both mom and child can attend simultaneously; will we have separate activities for children while the moms worship?

Many other people don't have fixed schedules, so we may want to reach out to people in real time or through live or recorded communications. These technologies can foster a sense of community through digital platforms and social networks. All of this is not to say that traditional services, regardless of the style of worship, don't have a place in our ministries. The importance is not to get bogged down in style or locations that become more important than the people we serve.

Our church recognized that it was becoming a sought-after gathering place for artists, writers, and other social groups. Our building was centrally located and highly recognizable. It was also convenient for people of all abilities to get to and to navigate inside. We took a break from looking at the usual thing that we thought our church should do, and instead considered ways to engage more fully with the community and the groups who were already reaching out to us. We now work with a number of groups to provide individual and group support services, art exhibitions, educational and business support services, and even more. When our conversations changed from worship style and management issues to community involvement, our entire outlook changed. Our church is doing better now than we had imagined, all because we listened to what the community needed and agreed to help in ways that were easy for us.

A tool that was created for large organizations to help them determine what their customers need and want from them is called Customer Scenario Mapping®. Customer Scenario Mapping® begins with people who are or who may be members and participants in our worship and other programs. This process involves personal communications with many of these individuals to find out their current needs and wants, both in and out of church. As a result of deep conversations and exploration, and through a professionally-facilitated workshop, churches (and other organizations) can determine what needs really exist in the community, and what items we can address quickly and effectively. This helps us also to create plans for the future that will yield significant benefits for the church and the community.

Customer Scenario Mapping® and programs like it keep us in tune with our actual mission and vision and how we respond to them, rather than take our existing programs and keep them active when they may no longer serve a purpose. For more information on this program, visit www.gods-business.com/resources.

A young yet highly-respected pastor decided to start his own church. This person had the support of another local congregation in terms of start-up funds and a location that was available. The pastor had significant experience in the mission field, and had no trouble reaching out to the community. The church did not succeed, though. This was probably due to two main reasons: One reason for starting the church was based on incorrect assumptions about worship styles driving success, and the second reason was that worship services focused only on the weekend. The congregation was not addressing the real issues behind why people were not going to church. With the model it used, the only way it would have succeeded is by taking members away from other local congregations.

Where

Digital versus In-Person

In today's world, our ministries are no longer dependent on a specific building or a specific geographical area. Therefore, as pastors and church leaders, we need to take a step back and figure out the best way for us to reach our target populations. In fact, it is possible that we could have a very effective ministry without meeting everyone (or anyone) in person.

Consider the ministry of Joel Olsten. He reaches roughly 16,000 people a week in person, but he reaches many times more people virtually though satellite radio, television broadcasts, printed materials, and other digital communications. Most of us are not looking to have this scale of ministry, but there are lessons we can learn from him: We can have very effective and loving ministries at our own level by using social media, podcasts, and other communication methods, as well as having our usual face-to-face interactions. In fact, even with traditional ministries, we can deepen our existing relationships with the people we serve by using technology so that we remain in more frequent two-way interactions. The point is not the means by which we communicate, but rather the intention and the love contained within that communication.

Geographical – Accessibility, Parking, Transportation

If our ministries are going to be tied to a specific geographical location, then we need to consider some important logistical considerations. Regardless of whether we are using a new building or an existing location to gather and to worship, we want our environment to allow our congregations to participate to the fullest extent possible. For example, if we truly want to be a welcoming organization, but we have a second floor and no elevator or wheelchair ramp, we almost certainly will not be able to reach everyone we want to.

In urban settings, where people may not have their own vehicle, we may need to consider other modes of transportation, i.e., public transportation. We also need to consider safety for all members, especially children, both in terms of the physical structure, i.e., no lead paint, as well as the community setting itself, i.e., safe areas to walk and to play. More about these specific topics and considerations can be found in the chapter on property management and building maintenance.

Our church is run quite well thanks to having a number of parishioners who are committed to Christ and who are also effective leaders in business and non-profit organizations outside of the church. Our programs are robust, and our congregation of about 140 people is very active. We have wanted to get over the 200 mark for several years. We have all the infrastructure we need to easily accomplish this except for one thing: parking. Our church is a historic building in an upper-class historic neighborhood. When the church was built in the late 1800s, it was a true community church; people walked from their homes in the neighborhood to come to church. Now, the congregation mostly commutes from other areas to get to church. The church does not have a parking lot, and there is no possibility of getting one since that would require the purchase and destruction of another historic building – something that the historical society would never allow. With only street parking available in a residential neighborhood, we really have an external limitation to our growth. We also cannot cater to people with physical disabilities very well due to the lack of parking and poor quality of the sidewalks – especially in the winter.

How

Probably, most of us consider the "how" of our ministry being a Sunday morning worship service. Regardless of the apparent success of our churches at this point, we cannot overlook the trends that an estimated 80% of our churches are in decline, and that Sunday morning worship is not the core of our civilization as it was even a few decades ago. The fact that fewer people are attending worship does not mean that the role of the church is different, but merely that how our churches do ministry needs to change.

All people still have the same inherent needs–food, safety, health, love, and the ability to flourish. The church's role is to help those in our midst to achieve each one of those needs and to hear the Good News through that service. Sunday morning worship may in fact distract some of us from what it is that we should be doing. As churches start to decline, they usually begin to argue amongst themselves about who is welcome and who is not, what kind of music should be done, and any other number of liturgical characteristics and faith-formation programs. The point is this: what we do needs to be meaningful to people both inside and outside of the church, and we need to do it to the best of our ability. Worship, including music and art, are more about taste–whereas our overall ministry is really about worshipping God by serving our neighbors. When our focus is inward, we are (or soon will be) in a state of decline. Only when our focus is outward can we truly grow and thrive.

The "how" then becomes the things that we do to serve our friends and our neighbors. Perhaps our ministries can be centered on education, community enrichment, healthy living, and evangelical lifestyles for our members outside of the church. This could lead us to focus more on programs such as after school education, nursery schools, life coaching, business coaching, and any number of marketplace ministries and community service. By focusing on these types of activities first and then using our worship experience as a way to not only thank God, but also to recharge ourselves, then our church will be empowered to make a

32

real difference far beyond our own walls. In fact, some of the most transformational churches don't have any walls at all!

Our church's sacred space is the streets of an inner city. Our congregation was originally created of homeless women and men, but has attracted non-homeless people as well. By meeting people where they are, literally, we show them that we really do care about them, and our ministry focuses on their daily needs. What a change in perspective it is when we read "Consider the Lilies" outside in the rain and without knowing where shelter and food will be available tomorrow. Our type of ministry is definitely for everyone. We do feel blessed not to have the burden of property so that we can focus on what we were really called to do. We are grateful to have support from churches with physical spaces and denominational resources, but we do know that even with nothing other than our voices and our love of God and neighbor, our church will keep going on, and keep making life better for those we serve, and also for ourselves.

Measuring Results – Cost/Benefit Analysis (ROI)

Any organization, whether it is a for-profit or a not-for-profit, measures the results of its programs and services by a cost/benefit analysis frequently referred to as a return on investment (ROI). It is crucial that we understand that cost does not only mean money. Cost also includes time, effort, and risk. Similarly, benefit does not necessarily mean that we have more people sitting in the pews on Sunday morning. The benefits we should be looking for are the transformations that we make in people's lives and in our community. For example, many people probably believe that marketing is a process in which we attract more people to come to our services and put more money in our plate. In that situation, ROI is seen as the number of people coming and the amount of money given; our success is only measured in numbers of individuals and cash collected.

If our church is truly God's Business, then ROI must be calculated very differently. How do our programs help people to have a deeper and more meaningful relationship with God and with each other? Consider a church that is trying to decide whether or not to keep a youth music program. Often church leaders would look at the number of children participating and how often (or how well) they would perform as being

34

the key measure of success. What they should be asking is how effective has the youth music program been at teaching the children about God, about Jesus, and what the stories in the Bible actually mean. The church leaders should also ask if the children's relationships with the other students and with the church at large become more solid. Also, have the parents of the children become more active and engaged with the church as well?

> *My church wanted to start some new outreach programs. The leadership team, and especially the Senior Pastor, adopted the idea that what we accomplished did not have to result in a higher church attendance. Our goal was to see measured success in community spirit, less unemployment, and fewer drug overdoses. Our direct impact on these things are a lot harder to measure that counting people or money, so we had to come up with ways to measure the success of the steps that we were taking that we believed would lead to accomplishing the stated goals. These issues are much bigger than anything our small congregation can accomplish on its own. By being an active participant in our*

community, though, we know that we are
really doing the important work while still
maintaining our worship and family
traditions.

In Summary

Marketing is about the strategy that our churches use to accomplish the vision and mission of the leaders (and, hopefully, the congregation, too). Marketing is not about promotion and evangelism; it is not about how we get more people in our church. Marketing is how we get our church into the community and how we can address the real needs of the people, not just the ones that we think they might have. Remember: marketing is an outside-in activity, not an inside-out activity. Only when we have a real understanding of community needs and a specific plan can we develop small groups, targeted ministries, and other programs that are useful and relevant. The programs and services that we offer are part of our ministries and operations function. They are the result of the marketing, not the marketing itself.

Chapter 3: Publicity, Communications, and Information Technology

Chapter Overview

Information technology is something that many pastors and church leaders don't give a lot of thought to. We all realize the value of individual communication components within our churches, but generally we don't have a real understanding of all the moving parts. Some churches have been forward-thinking enough to have a ministry dedicated to digital communication and information technology as a whole. This chapter provides an overview of the various systems that we all have or most likely will have in the near future. Information technology, including the systems that we use for publicity and all other communications, is instrumental for our successful ministries now and into the future.

Information technology is the use and the study of the systems that people and organizations use for storing, retrieving, and sending information. These systems can be computers, telephones, audio systems, video conferencing, security systems, and wearable devices, and even more types of digital communication platforms. The way that people and organizations communicate becomes more intricate every day. - Paraphrased from the Merriam-Webster Dictionary

Audio Systems

One of my favorite television shows was an English comedy called "Bless Me Father". In one of the episodes, the church got a new microphone that the priest could wear around his neck. Unfortunately, he forgot to turn off the microphone before he went into the confessional and began hearing confessions. Just like in that episode, even after many decades of having sound amplification systems in our churches, many of our churches still don't get sound systems quite right. The objective is to use technology to communicate clearly and effectively, yet, in many cases, the technology that we use fails to meet its objective either because of user error or technology error. In these cases, our message becomes distorted or lost entirely. It's important to remember that the quality of our communication (the content AND the technological system) is often one of the first impressions that our church makes. If we have problems with distortion, feedback, or other failures, it distracts from the worship experience and our ability to ministry effectively to regulars and guests alike.

Even before we get to the technology aspect, we need to think about the people we entrust with our communication systems. Many churches rely on the grace of volunteers to run our sound systems during worship. We are grateful for those volunteers, and they are an important part of our community. Even so, imagine what happens when we select someone to run our audio ministry who has no proper training on the equipment or sound engineering in general, or who themselves have problems with their own hearing.

In the case of audio systems in worship, the objective is to have the sound evenly distributed through the church, at a comfortable level, and not to make everything as loud as possible. Therefore, when we put in new equipment or try new methods of sound engineering, it is wise to have a professional come in and guide us through the process. By making good impressions in worship and communication, the people that we are trying to reach can focus in on the message of God and not the idiosyncrasies of the technology and the people running it. We all know of situations where friends and family have gone to a wedding at a different church and came back with horror stories or amusing anecdotes about the quality of the musician and singers. Similar stories occur when sound systems crash or otherwise malfunction in a way that detracts from the worship and celebration. In this regard, the people operating the sound systems are no less important than the people leading worship.

When evaluating the needs of our congregation and our outreach, the importance of hiring experts in the audio/visual field to advise us cannot be stressed enough. Most churches are not blessed with seasoned and licensed experts who can architect audio and video systems from scratch using wired or wireless systems. Most audio volunteers likely do not understand the implications of how they impact or interfere with the ministries of music, lighting, and so forth.

Cost and quality of these systems vary greatly, and even the best quality and highest cost equipment can still fail the church and its mission if it is not installed or operated properly. Churches should never be ashamed to reach out for expert help, but rather they should rejoice in the opportunity to work with experts who can create reliable systems that operate easily. We should all be able to celebrate and worship God in a way that is inspirational to the participants and worthy of God's praise.

God said to Aaron that he should offer a bull without blemish as a burnt offering. Similarly, we should offer our best selves in worship and in life as a worthy tribute to God. Mediocrity should never be the goal. - Leviticus 9:2 (Paraphrased)

Video Communications

Video communications can be used in a number of different ways. This can make our worship and outreach activities more robust and more engaging, yet there are a number of important things to consider. First, let's look at the use of video recording during worship services. Many of us recognize the value of recording our worship service so we can include people who are homebound, away at college, or in other remote locations. We want them to have the opportunity to experience worship through digital files or live streaming. We should note that a number of churches consider recorded or broadcasted worship services to be a form of evangelism, yet it is extremely rare that this is actually successful in terms of transforming lives or increasing in-person attendance. Therefore, when we consider recording our services, we need to think through what our real objective is and then create systems that reflect the accomplishment of that objective. It is important to know that there can be significant expense in acquiring

41

the right equipment and expertise to make a quality recording or broadcast, including the engineering, "packaging," and hosting. Additionally, there are copyright implications that cannot be ignored. We will talk more about this later in this chapter.

When thinking about the time and expense of recorded or broadcast worship services, we have to be realistic about the number of people we will be reaching. We need to consider whether or not another solution, perhaps a more low-tech solution, will be better for the people that we are trying to reach. However, if our churches are looking to do different kinds of ministries and that is in keeping with their vision and mission, then it may be strategically useful to record worship services or segments of worship services that can be distributed safely, effectively, and more cost effectively. In these cases, you may want to look at ministries using podcasts, YouTube videos, or other social media platforms. The equipment that would be most appropriate for these outlets may not be the same equipment we would need if we were to record entire worship services for other channels like cable television. An excellent example of this is the Joel Olsten ministry on SiriusXM®. In these satellite radio programs, there are approximately 25 minutes of captivating content in the form of a message by Joel, as well as a way for the listeners to connect back to the ministry itself. However, in these particular programs, there is no music performed, there are not specific prayer requests, and there are no other personal announcements that would identify specific people or entities. This is a great benchmark for our churches if we consider doing the same type of broadcasting. I encourage you to explore and watch/listen to your favorite worship services online or via other media. Consider which ones you think inspire you the most. Like a good TedTalk, you will probably find that the message is between 15-20 minutes in length, makes two or three salient points, and leads you with a call to action. You will also find a real understanding and concern for the privacy of the individuals in the congregation and listening audience.

This one country church had two services each Sunday. At the earlier service, there was this person who stood up to share announcements every single week. Now it was the custom to pass around the microphone so that people could say the person's name and perhaps a brief description of what was going on with the person. However, this one particular individual would stand up, ask for prayers for an individual using that person's first and last name, even though that person was

43

not part of the community. The really bad part is that the announcement / prayer request would then go on to describe very personal details about the person. Once, it was even announced that so-and-so was wrestling with a drug addiction problem. Unfortunately, our church broadcast its worship services on community cable television. This person's information, whether it was true or not, was now "out there" and there was no taking it back.

Regardless of the type of media broadcasting, whether it is live broadcasts or recorded messages, we need to keep people's anonymity and safety in the forefront of our minds. When I have mentioned this issue and some stories to colleagues and other pastors, they frequently have said, "Oh my, I have never thought of that."

Written Communications

Sermons have been recorded in writing for hundreds of years. Today, it is the norm that we share our sermons and messages not only in the context of worship, but also emails, newsletters, blog posts, Facebook posts, and almost any other form of social media. The internet has opened up infinite possibilities for us to share messages of God's grace and love. In proportion to the ease of communication, the elements of risk have also increased proportionally. Intentional or unintentional plagiarism and copyright infringement are all too easy. The possibility of accidentally harming other people by widely sharing information that should be held close to home is also a distinct possibility. In fact, this happens in church, in business, and in personal lives more than we care to admit. Digital communication is an extremely powerful tool, but as with any other powerful tool that has the potential for great good, there is also the potential to create extreme damage.

One of the goals of written communication is to keep in close contact with congregation members in between worship services and other in-person activities. Email, digital newsletters, texting, and so forth all allow us instant or almost instant channels of communication with one person or a group of people. Newsletters are perhaps the most formal of these communications and, therefore, usually have the least amount of risk. This is due to the fact that they are clearly written, reviewed, and evaluated before they get sent out. Newsletters are typically created by a team with an intentional message, and the team approach to communication is normally done in a thoughtful manner. Email can be a little riskier. It is possible to send the wrong message when we reply hastily because of our being in a rush or being distracted. Our intentions may be helped slightly if emoticons are used, but it is all too common that the reader interprets a different tone to our message than we intended. That can have unintended consequences in businesses and in churches. In ministry, misinterpreted notes or messages can be damaging or even hurtful.

For example, a good practice is to never send an email right away, but to let it sit a moment or two and then come back to it before sending it. If your response is of a highly personal nature to you or to the other person, it is wise to reread it carefully before sending. No matter how much care we put into a first draft, we undoubtedly will make some changes when we re-read a message whether it is for something simple like a spelling mistake or because of a lack of clarity. Additionally, it is important to recognize the dangers of "replying to all" instead of just replying to the sender alone when multiple people are included on an email string.

In terms of interactive social media like Facebook, we need to take special precautions. In today's world, regardless of whatever position we or our churches take on any number of issues, and regardless of how loving or true to the gospel we try to be, you know that at least half of the population will be strongly against our view. Even if, for example, it is just one person's comment that gets posted on our Facebook timeline, a firestorm of angry replies can be directed at our church, our

46

community, or an individual, specifically creating a flow of communication that neither builds up the kingdom of God or our personal relationships.

As with audio and visual communications, we also need to be sensitive to the anonymity and needs of others by not posting anything about anybody in the form of text, pictures, or audio without their specific permissions. This may be counter-intuitive to the way most churches currently use Facebook. When it is our members and our church at stake, however, we must mitigate the risk of negative feelings, inappropriate actions, and even legal implications. A good rule of thumb is "when in doubt, don't post it."

> *Our church made a real effort to become a "digital safe space" much like we try to be a safe place physically. Cyber bullying has become a real issue for not only the youth in our community, but for adults as well. Broken relationships of different types are often behind this, but not always. Sometimes simply having a different opinion than someone else in terms of theological understanding, social norms, and demographics can trigger a backlash from anonymous or known sources online.*

We also have come to realize that it is possible for people to be "tagged" in other people's photos posted on social media. These pictures may be amusing to some people, but they can also be extremely damaging to others. Would those of us who are adults and church leaders today really want every aspect of our lives as youths and young adults (or even older adults) posted online and commented on? Therefore, we wanted to protect those in our midst and our broader community. Our church no longer posts any pictures of individuals or groups without specific permission. We also do not post any comments on the church social media about anything, regardless of how "centrist" we think it is. We also try to keep our settings so that comments cannot be posted without our reviewing them first. If we don't do this, the time we would probably lose fixing social media issues would outweigh all of the positive things that we have done for our community.

A Note on Copyright Law

Broadcasting via the internet has made opportunities for our ministry much greater than ever before. Our natural ambition may be to reach as many people as possible, and to provide a fun and engaging experience with them both online and in person. For small churches and organizations, and especially for individuals, it is easy and tempting to use information that has already been created by someone else. Be very careful with how you distribute other people's information. No matter what, always give people credit for their work and creativity. Even then, giving credit to the source may not always be sufficient to meet copyright laws. We have all heard about video and music privacy in the secular world that turns a blind eye to the thinkers and artists who created this content. We are not immune to piracy in our sacred places as either.

"Thou Shall Not Steal"

Or photocopy choir music...

Or broadcast music performed in church...

Or plagiarize texts...

Or include copyrighted images in PowerPoints...

Or play recorded music for worship services without permission...

- *Paraphrased from Deuteronomy 5:19*

One of the most frequent issues churches have with copyright law involves music. There are two distinct areas that warrant our conversation. First is the reproduction of printed music for our congregation and singers. Second is the performance of copyrighted music in our worship services, especially when our services are recorded or broadcast. Copyright laws prohibit unauthorized usage of a great deal of printed and recorded music. However, this probably still happens more than we would care to admit. The moral and ethical issues surrounding this situation are self-evident and do not need to be discussed in this book. We will mention some of the legal implications, however. Although it has been rare, it is still possible for our churches and staff to be held liable regarding copyright laws. Even if our church as a whole is not aware of and does not condone the use of unauthorized music, the actions of a single employee could put the church at risk. Do we really want to risk our financial assets and other property to save a few dollars on printed or recorded music?

Also, consider the implications for the controversy that would likely ensue between the employee and the church if such a case would ever be brought. All in all, there is no excuse for the unauthorized use of music—ever! Remember that music written by contemporary composers is also under copyright in terms of broadcasting. That means when we do an audio or video recording of our worship services, the music that our musicians perform becomes a public performance once it is recorded and broadcast. In fact, in concert situations, the music is also considered to be a public performance, and therefore subject to copyright laws.

There are a number of resources available where we can obtain copyright licenses for the reproduction of printed music and music performance. It is important to know that no one resource can provide us with a license for all composers and publishers. In most cases our churches will end up with two, and sometimes three, licenses in order to perform and record all of the music we want to perform in the context of worship. Check our resources list for some useful information, or explore Copyright laws online or with a legal professional.

Computer and Database Systems

Most churches today have some sort of computer system that is used by clergy and staff for document creation and management, email communications, and membership databases. These systems may reside on hard drives or portable drives within the church. Nowadays, they may also be hosted in the cloud. The solution that is best for you depends on your needs, now and in the future. There are advantages and disadvantages for each. Outside experts are your best resource to evaluate your computer systems needs in terms of speed, memory, usability, cost, and data security.

We may think that the data we keep about our members and churches in general is of no value to anyone else. The fact of the matter is that personal information and corporate information can be used in nefarious ways by people who should not have it. Hospitals and health care companies are obligated to operate by HIPAA laws that strongly protect personal information. Although our churches are not held to these standards, HIPAA provides a good touchstone for us to use as an example when setting our own information security standards. A best practice is to keep as little information about our members as necessary, without sacrificing their engagement with us or their safety.

Other people may consider our office system to be really outdated. However, we intentionally keep our staff and congregation records, as well as our church management systems, in a computer that is not attached to the internet. Our thinking is that if that computer is not attached to the internet, then it will never get hacked unless someone breaks into the church office and guesses the password and unique user identifiers. In a case like this, we would have a pretty good guess about who took the information anyway.

We do have other computers and office equipment that are online that we use for communication – email, social media, etc. However, no personal data about our congregation is stored or transmitted on these devices. We also have a strict policy on which staff members and volunteers have access to church or personal email on our system, and only a couple of designated people have any internet access on church equipment at all.

In general, our churches should be very careful about how we assign email addresses and computer access to paid staff and volunteers. Church policy should be clearly stated pertaining to email, computer access, and internet access. Appropriate behavior and church expectations for communication associated in any way with the church needs to be clearly defined and enforced. In today's world, this simply can't be overstated. The reputation of your church, your belief systems, and your staff and volunteers hinges on your digital presence remaining safe and unblemished.

Even with our best attempts to keep our digital systems secure, there is always an element of risk both internally and externally. Systems that monitor all activity on our computers may be worth the investment depending upon the level of exposure we have. Consider getting a computer system security evaluation, and see some of our helpful free resources online.

Security Systems

Many churches have different beliefs on the need for and level of security on church property. In a perfect world, our churches would reflect our faith by staying open all the time and welcoming everybody. However, that may not be the right response depending on our geographic location and the motives of people inside or outside the church. Some people really do intend to cause physical, emotional, or financial harm to other people and organizations. While our job is to minister and to serve the larger community, our role as pastors and church leaders includes keeping everyone safe to the best of our ability while they are in our care. Therefore, it is appropriate and expected that we are prepared to monitor, prevent, and respond to dangerous situations.

Security systems, whether they be entry alarm systems, fire alarm systems, water level alarm systems, or anything else, require electronic connectivity to a main station within the church and often to a central monitoring location. Many security systems involve monitoring offices which are remote and usually hosted by a third party. The effectiveness of these systems depends on adequate planning, installation, and management. More about this can be seen in the chapter about buildings and maintenance.

Telecommunications

It is amazing to see how far telephones have come along technologically in the last relatively few years. The need for highly complex phone systems within a church is often no longer necessary thanks to the prevalence and affordability of wireless communication systems. People frequently communicate using video as well as audio for both social and business reasons. Our ministries can potentially benefit from this technology as well. Teleconferencing and video conferencing solutions can be a reasonable and viable alternative to face-to-face committee meetings where it is often difficult to get all the leaders together at the same place at the same time. Video conferencing solutions can potentially also be used for small group activities and other appropriate small group communication depending upon the needs of the church and the congregation. As with other technologies, determining the best overall solution for your church depends upon your present and future needs and your financial resources.

The church that I work for is in the Northeast. A couple of times every winter, we usually get too much snow or ice for us to have staff and members come to church safely. One week we hosted worship via live streaming over the internet. We had a couple of technical issues at first, and it was really strange seeing worship performed in an empty church, but overall the people who "attended" had a good experience. Some said that even though there was no music, no choir, and no congregation in the feed, they still felt included and that they had a more meaningful experience than either not going to church at all or watching some televangelist.

It is important to note that, although most of us can freely access information online, we do need to be mindful of how people with disabilities can access the information that we present digitally. People who are blind, for example, can navigate the internet reasonably well, but only if we use the technology that is already available to us that provides image descriptions, navigation descriptions, and other audio assistance. This is important for more than just our websites. We need to make sure that all media are set up in a way that people can navigate our resources even without the use of vision. Similarly, we need to consider that audio files should have captioning with them if it is at all reasonable to do so. We need to remember whom we are ministering to and make sure we remove any barriers that get in their way of them fully engaging with us. You can find out more about online accessibility in our free resources or by talking with accessibility experts.

We came to realize that having audio options online not only made sense for someone who was visually impaired in our group, but that others liked being able to listen to the audio while they were driving or at work. Whether you have a disability or not, sometimes it is just really useful to be able to listen to a message instead of having to read it.

Online Banking

Some churches have begun to incorporate digital banking services in lieu of or in addition to the usual way of collecting money in a basket or plate during an offertory. Online giving can be a reasonable way to round out the peaks and valleys in a congregation's revenue stream. This doesn't mean that your church needs a credit card machine in the Sanctuary. However, you can seriously consider having people use online giving plans through their own banks. Services like PayPal can be a viable alternative to in-church electronic payment systems. Options like this can provide greater data security for both the giver and the receiver. In some ways, the hardest part about giving money to the church online is dealing with the perceptions about each other that may arise in worship. When the basket is passed for a church service and people appear not to appear to contribute anything, there could be some unintentional judgment happening, even though these people are already pledging online.

> *The church that I am at has some people that pledge and give to the church online only. Their argument seems to be that they are truly committed to the church, and they don't ever want to miss a payment even if they are away. They have a check automatically drawn from their account and mailed to the church every week. We have some others that are quite regular in their online giving as well. To accommodate everybody, our church provides a printed-note that says "Online Pledge" that a person can place in the basket in the event that there may be someone watching (and judging). I would like to just have everyone pay electronically, and have people put written*

58

prayer requests into the plate instead. That way we can say thanks over the prayers instead of the cash during the Doxology.

In Summary

Information technology systems can grow to vast proportions quickly, and they can become highly complex. Churches will generally be more successful with their IT systems if they work intentionally with experts who have proven experience in a broad range of digital communication. Some churches have a dedicated ministry for this type of service. A person in this role may be easily distracted by the technology itself. However, even a communications or an IT minister must maintain a clear focus on the vision and mission of the church. Otherwise IT may inadvertently become more important than pastoral care.

As with all the other topics covered in this book, it can be easy to get bogged down in the details. It is important to remember that IT is only a tool for our ministries. In and of itself, IT has no value. Only the Good News and our service to others have actual value. IT is important in how it allows us to communicate with the community and how we use it to keep our members safe and engaged.

Chapter 4: Security & Safety

Chapter Overview

Most of us will hopefully never experience senseless and extreme acts of violence in our churches. However, we cannot assume that such an event will never happen to us. Like texting and driving, we cannot pretend that our situation is inherently different and that we will always be safe (lucky). Simply put, we are morally obliged to keep our congregations and staff members safe to the best of our ability. That means we need to have plans in place for a variety of safety and security issues. These include natural and manmade disasters, acts of extreme violence, and protection against online and offline bullying and stalking. Similarly, we must be prepared for health emergencies at our churches which may take place during or after office hours, or even during worship services.

Our churches play an important role for our congregations and communities. By working with law enforcement agencies, specialized trainers, and community leaders, we can create detailed plans about how the church will respond to dangerous events which are out of our control. These plans may not only help protect church property, but also prepare our members for how to take care of themselves and others in an emergency. Plans and drills will help all members know exactly what to do in the event of an emergency or threat of violence at the church.

This chapter will highlight a number of safety and security issues facing our churches and the communities that they serve. It will also provide a checklist for security measures, sample items for your policy and procedure manual, and some useful insights and experiences from top security experts.

Church Evacuations

Most of us remember the fire drills that we had back in school. Although these may have been looked on lightly by us as young students, they remain the best tool for making sure that large groups of people have a plan and have practiced exactly what to do in order to evacuate a building quickly and safely.

If your church has not developed an emergency evacuation plan and provided training to it members, youth, and visitors, then it is imperative that you make this a top priority. This is in fact a relatively easy program to implement, but it must not be delayed since an emergency can happen at any time. In many cases, your local law enforcement and fire departments will happily help you to create a plan and may even help you conduct the drills.

Once the evacuation plan has been created, drills should be conducted at least once a year. However, if you have a high volunteer, staff, or member turn-over, you may need to conduct drills more often. The goal of the evacuation drill is to assess the level of understanding of the evacuation procedure by staff, members, and guests. Issues that arise during the drill will indicate areas that need to be refined or re-taught. More specifically, drills will:

- Identify problems with the evacuation plan
- Test alterations or changes to the existing evacuation procedure
- Help new staff, volunteers, members, and guests with the procedure
- Confirm that people with special needs or disabilities can be evacuated quickly and safely

Remember that if you have multiple buildings, then each building should have its own evacuation plan and drills. Keep in mind that even if a building has multiple exits, plans and drills should be conducted as if only one egress was available because of fire or other damage. Remember, there must always be a plan of action for helping the disabled, even if stairs or other obstacles are involved.

It is recommended that outside experts or appointed observers from within the church are used to pay close attention to what happens during the drills. Specifically, they should look for:

- How fire wardens or other leaders execute their positions
- Problems with opening doors both inside the building as well as the final exits
- Issues for children or disabled persons
- Inappropriate actions by the evacuees including going back for personal items, using elevators, or not closing windows and doors as people leave.
- The use of the best escape route vs. more common circulation flows
- Issues with communication during and after the evacuation, including the roll call
- Issues with tracking evacuees to ensure everyone has gotten out of the building safely

Once a drill has been completed, all participants should have the opportunity to share their feedback. The fire wardens or other leaders should also file a report confirming the results of the drill, and any remedial actions that are deemed necessary should be implemented.

For more information, please see our free online resources or connect with emergency response professionals in your community.

Preparing for Natural Disasters

Regardless of where the church is located, our buildings and congregations are probably at risk for some type of natural emergency or disaster from time to time. Flooding, hurricanes, tornadoes, wildfires, and ice and snow can all potentially threaten our congregations.

Hopefully you already have disaster plans in place. If you don't, a good place to start is to contact your local planning or geologist departments to find out if your property is located in any particular risk zone (floods, landslides, etc.). You should also be aware of any community emergency plans, warning systems, and evacuation routes. Our churches not only need this information for our staff, volunteers, and members, but we can also serve our community at large by helping to share information and support in preparing for this kind of event.

The checklist below is appropriate not only for your church, but it should also be shared with the staff, volunteers, and members so that everyone can be suitably prepared at church and at home for significant national emergencies:

- Plan your evacuation routes in case you are ordered to leave the community.
- Coordinate with a point person who is a significant distance from your area to act as the

emergency contact person. He or she will be the person who can get in touch with everyone in case people get separated during an emergency or natural disaster. Make sure that everyone knows who this person is and has all of their contact information.

- Ensure that home-bound, disabled, or anyone with special needs is taken care of. Local authorities should be notified, and there should be people appointed to make sure that they will be protected or evacuated as needed.

- Prepare to minimize hazards in and around buildings. Turn off the electricity when there is standing water or downed power lines. If possible, gas and water supplies should also be turned off before an evacuation. All large outside items should be secured.

- Remember to keep a sufficient number of fire extinguishers on hand at all times.

- If your church has a basement or below-grade areas, then consider installing sump pumps and backup power supplies.

- Fuel tanks should be anchored regardless if they are inside or outside of the building. The fuel can contaminate the building, and the tank itself could damage other property if it becomes dislodged.

In the event that an evacuation from the area is required, there are some important items for you and your congregation to have ready to take along. These items are crucial for your safety, security, and peace of mind.

- Cash, checkbook, credit cards, debit cards, phone calling cards
- Banking and investment information
- Health insurance information / medical cards
- Minimum of one month's supply of all medications plus prescription information
- Birth certificates and Social Security cards
- Medical records
- Driver's license, photo identification, passports
- Foreign national identification (green card, immigration papers, work permits)
- Marriage certificate, divorce papers, child custody orders, other personal legal documents
- School records
- Property deeds, rental/lease agreements
- Car title, registration, and insurance information
- Keys: House, Car, Safety deposit box, Post Office box
- Cellphone, charger, and adaptor

For more information, please see our free online resources or connect with emergency response professionals in your community.

Health Emergencies

No matter the demographics of our congregations, health emergencies can occur at any time, including during worship. Undoubtedly, many of you have already encountered this type of event in your ministry. Although we cannot make plans for every type of emergency, we can set up policies and procedures that will help to protect the affected person as well as the staff and congregation. We must also keep in mind that pastors, worship leaders, and other staff may be incapacitated at any time, and therefore a well thought-out plan must be in place so that all aspect of the church's mission may be continued relatively seamlessly.

An effective way to ensure that church operations work in spite of unexpected personnel emergencies is to have all processes and activities of the church documented, along with contact information for key leaders. Contingency plans should also be rehearsed, much like any other drill. This level of planning is not only effective for emergency situations, but also to helps an organization to understand how vacation time or other extended absences can be handled with minimal impact.

Consider what could happen to your church if the senior pastor (perhaps you) of a church were to fall seriously ill during a worship service and is incapacitated for a number of weeks. Who would the person be that automatically steps into your role to see that worship continues? Who would be the people who would know how to care for you during a health crisis? How would your family be notified in case you happened to be alone that day? This book will not delve into local or broader denominational policy which may or may not effectively handle a situation that requires immediate attention. Rather, the goal is to have you think clearly about everything that would need to happen, and who would be the specific person or people (not necessarily those who fill a specific role or have a specific title) that would fill in for you at the drop of a hat. On a high level, here are some of the things that you and your congregation need in place:

Liturgical Leadership:

If the pastor is the person who oversees all aspects of worship, then special attention to detail is required to prepare for an unexpected absence whether it be short-term or long-term. The following questions provide a starting point for clearly outlining what will happen at your church in this situation.

- Who handles the preaching and other worship responsibilities if the pastor suddenly falls ill?
- Will the worship service be temporarily stopped due to medical attention that is required in the worship service, and then be resumed to its completion with a different leader? Or will the

congregation be dismissed if the pastor is taken away for emergency care?

• What will be the protocol in terms of audio and video during a medical emergency? Will the expectation be that amplification and recording is stopped immediately? Who is the person that is authorized to make that decision on the spot?

• If the pastor is incapacitated for a number of weeks, which person will have the distinct responsibility to make sure that worship services continue during this time? Remember that having a committee to do this is not enough – there must be a singular person who is accountable. That person may be the head of a committee, however, and should involve many other people, yet he or she must have the authority and the accountability while the pastor is unavailable.

Church Operations:

If the pastor is the acting manager for church operations, then there must be a clear and documented description of each activity that the pastor is responsible for. There also needs to be documented policy and procedures for who in the church will be held accountable for each activity and a description of how these activities can be performed successfully. The following questions will guide you through the thought process required to create a plan in the event that your church does not already have one.

• Which person or group of people is responsible for staff management? Are there specific people or positons that are responsible for managing paid and volunteer staff? If an issue arises with employee or volunteer performance while the pastor is incapacitated, how will that situation be handled?

• Which person or group of people is responsible for fiscal management? Are there people authorized to write checks or make other payments on the church's behalf without the pastor's signature? What are the checks and balances for fiscal management in the absence of pastoral oversight?

• How are office hours to be handled in the absence of the pastor? Are there enough staff members and trained volunteers to effectively handle incoming communications? Will office hours need to be modified? Will office staff and volunteers have access to an organizational chart clearly stating the person responsible for each activity in case they have questions or need to get someone else's questions answered?

• Who is responsible for notifying the pastor's family in the event that they are not present? How will access to accurate contact information be handled?

• Who is responsible for notifying other church or denominational leaders (if necessary)? Can other local clergy be called in to assist with pastoral care activities?

70

• If the pastor lived alone at the time of the emergency, who will be responsible for maintaining his or her residence? This may include feeding pets, retrieving mail, and responding to property issues that come up. Keeping track of the pastor's vehicle may also be helpful depending on the circumstances.

Many of these questions, and some others, can also be taken into consideration for other staff and volunteer positions.

There may be a higher likelihood that we will encounter a parishioner, rather than a staff member, having a health emergency at church. With people frequently staying single or becoming single again in our society, it is quite possible that situations like this may arise for single people of most any age. In these cases, the church should be ready to step up to help the person receive the care that they need. Anyone who has ever been physically impaired, even for a relatively short time, knows the value of having a support network to help with even basic activities like transportation, shopping, house chores and the like.

At one of our worship services, a member started having some medical issues. Fortunately, we have an EMT in the congregation who took notice and went to sit with her. This person did not want any help, but it became obvious that her condition was worsening. In spite of trying to help her out of the Sanctuary, she refused to leave. This was causing a fair amount of stress for the worship leaders and other parishioners who by this time became aware of what was going on. When the person finally agreed to receiving help, 911 had already been called. She was quickly taken to the hospital for treatment.

The situation was a bit complicated because she was the only caregiver for her husband who was essentially home-bound. Even though someone from the church tried to call him, there was no answer by phone. The church had no record of the phone numbers and addresses of their adult children, so we were at a loss about how to get the family involved. Also, this lady's car had to stay in the church lot because nobody had a way to bring it to her home for her. All this made us realize that it's not just youth that we need emergency contact information for. Elderly people should also provide the church with a list of people to call in case anything like this happens again.

Bullying, Stalking, and Personal Violence

It seems that more attention has been given to cyber bullying over the last few years, and with good reason. The internet has created very efficient ways for people to overtly and covertly threaten people and generally make their lives miserable. Note, however, that in-person actions like bullying, stalking, and other threats of personal violence are still all too common.

One of our objectives as a congregation and as congregational leaders is to make every effort to keep people safe when they are engaging with us. This may be done by observing good practices when people are at the church (providing windows in all meeting rooms, security systems, key management, etc.), but we also must make every effort that we provide "digital" safe spaces as well. We cannot focus solely on preventing physical harm in person while ignoring the very real possibility of someone being the victim of emotional and psychological harm via digital communications.

In our church, we had one young woman and her daughter come to worship with us. They became regulars at the church over the course of several weeks. It turns out that

73

they had to leave home and had put a restraining order on her husband. The mom was obviously very concerned about staying under the radar, so to speak, but felt a real need for her and her daughter to be a part of a worshipping community.

Fortunately, some of our leadership team had thought this type of situation through prior to these folks visiting us. It seems that a similar issue had come up at another church where one of our leaders had served. Because of that, we do not do video broadcasts of our services. No photos or videos are taken, either, without the specific consent. And we never take pictures of children without parental permission. We understand the damage that can be done to people unintentionally. The technology available today is simply too powerful and too quick for us to stay ahead of it as an organization. So we err on the side of extreme caution – especially with our social media presence and also with any media publicity that we get at our events.

Digital technology today provides amazing resources for our ministries. We can share God's love with others in ways that were unthinkable even a generation ago. However, these technologies provide the same level of opportunities for people with nefarious intentions. People want to socialize online. We want to publicize our churches and ministries online. And we know that pictures and videos make for more interesting websites and Facebook pages. There are real risks involved when we make the decision to put our churches and our messages online. Understanding these risks and mitigating them to keep our people and our ministries safe is something that must not be overlooked. Too many church leaders take a weak stance on personal privacy of the members. Unless these leaders would want their own picture and personal information (and negative comments from "trolls") put on billboards across town, they should make every effort not to do the same to others on a global scale.

For further information about digital security and best practices, go to www.gods-business.com/resources.

Active Shooters

"This is a tragedy that no community should have to experience. It is senseless. It is unfathomable that someone would walk into a church when people are having a prayer meeting and take their lives."

-Police Chief Mullen of Charleston, SC

Violence against churches is nothing new. From the very beginning of Christianity, assemblies of believers have been targeted with violence and even death. Over time, conflict has arisen from both inside and outside of the church. Modern weaponry has only changed some of the methods of violence, but not the cause or the harm done by it. In today's world, it is inexcusable for us not to have a policy and a plan for our church to handle active shooters or other extreme acts of violence. We simply must be prepared for how we can keep our congregations safe should anything like this ever happen at our churches.

Remember that the intention of this book is not to put a moral stake in the ground on any issue. The fact is that many churches would never want weaponry of any kind brought onto the premises. Others, however, may be perfectly comfortable with concealed or open carry policies at church. The point is that our churches need to have a policy about what to do if something happens. A state of crisis is not the time to hatch out a plan to keep people safe. As leaders who are responsible for the entire wellbeing of others, we simply must have these difficult conversations, preferably with some level of external expert advice.

"Facilities designated as 'Gun Free Zones' only prevent the law abiding person from carrying a gun on the premises. I will also state that not every permit-holder should

76

intervene in such a situation. But I would argue that promoting premises as "Gun Free Zones" is just advertising the fact that a perpetrator will not meet any armed resistance in this facility. Is this one of many reasons these types of zones are chosen by a perpetrator to commit these type of acts? In almost all of these incidents, the perpetrator commits suicide once they are met with armed resistance/police, often at just the arrival of the police."

-Tactical Defense Training Center

The issue of firearms is not the only thing that should be discussed in terms of personal safety. Self-defense disciplines can also cause grave harm to others. Knowing when and how far to use these skills should be determined ahead of time. Learning how to recognize different types and levels of threats, and the most effective ways to deal with them, can save us a great deal of heartache in the future.

Our peaceful religions exist in a violent world. Determining the best way to mitigate threats while remaining true to our belief system is not an easy process. Ignoring the problem, however, is not an option. For resources that can help you with planning and strategies for safety, go to www.gods-business.com/resources.

In Summary

This chapter is intended to provide a jumping-off point for pastors and church leaders to start discussing ways that congregations can and will react in times of crisis. Jesus ministered to people in need, often at the darkest times of their lives. Our churches, too, are responsible for having ministries that are effective in both calm and crisis. Having a discipline of being aware, prepared, and responsive to a variety of situations, good and bad, makes church leaders and congregations a resource that God can use effectively no matter what.

Chapter 5: Staff Recruiting and Development

Chapter Overview

What is management? Management involves the activities associated with running an organization, such as controlling, leading, monitoring, organizing, and planning. Management and leadership sometimes get confused because the terms are often interchanged. However, there is a big difference. For the purpose of this book, we affirm that leadership is the skillset used to bring an organization somewhere new; management is the skillset used to keep existing programs and operations working smoothly.

Mature ministries will invariably need paid or volunteer staff or both. For those pastors who are starting a church from scratch, they may have the luxury of selecting all of their staff right from the start. Others who are placed into existing churches may have to learn to work with many of the staff members and volunteers who are already in place. In some denominations, the pastor has no control over the hiring and firing of the staff. In other places, the pastor has complete authority. In either case, it is the role of the pastor and any other church leaders that are involved in staff relations and development to identify, attract, train, and retain staff that can help guide the church in accordance with its vision and mission.

It is not wise to assume that the most highly-trained and qualified staff members are ordained clergy. Similarly, it is not a good idea to assume that church leaders who are older, or have more longevity in the institution, have more wisdom than others. The power dynamic can be a very tricky thing to deal with in churches, perhaps even more so than in regular businesses. This is because we come to church with the assumption that everyone shares the same vision and mission. In fact, there is a lot of fluidity within Christianity and even within denominations and individual churches.

It is worth noting that there are personalities that do not work well with others. It is only reasonable that we should expect that, at some point during our ministerial career, we will encounter toxic personalities. This chapter will provide us with some resources to work with these dysfunctional personalities and at the same time to keep the best interest of the church and other people at heart.

It is not uncommon that these people are very quick to volunteer and offer advice to others who are in leadership, sometimes even on their first visit to the church.

This chapter will help avoid some pitfalls of organizational stress and conflict so that you may transition effectively from a role of management to that of a leader.

Personality Assessments and Background Checks

Personality Assessment

There are a number of proven tools that are available that may help us understand our own personalities and those of others. In too many churches, these tools or methods are seen as a luxury item and unnecessary for the effective management of a church. In fact, we should look at personality assessment tools as an absolute necessity for at least the senior leadership team, as well as other people in various professional and volunteer positions. Personality assessments help us to understand how to effectively interact with each other, and to reap the maximum benefit from the individual personalities on our team.

The types of things that we can learn from personality assessments include whether some people are more socially oriented or more task oriented. Also, some are focused more on other peoples' feelings (the soft skills) or on getting the job done (hard skills). Some people may typically process things more slowly (need all the information and extra time to process the information) than others. Or they may respond to things quickly (making quick decisions). Each combination of personality attributes has its own set of strengths and potential areas of growth. When people become stressed, what is typically their personal strengths can turn into liabilities. Being in tune with the personalities and tendencies of your staff and volunteers can help you guide the behaviors, feelings, and tasks more efficiently.

One church had completed the search for a new pastor. Overwhelmingly, people in the congregation wanted someone exactly like the person who had just left (only younger of course). The problem is that the church has been steadily declining in attendance over the last decade. Although there are a number of youth who have started participating at church, their parents are generally not involved. If you were to break down the congregation according to age, there would be very few (probably about six percent) who are in the 25 to 55-year-old range. Some leaders are starting to recognize that the church will not be viable within 10 years because of the current demographics.

The previous minister created deep and lasting relationships with the members, and even created a program or two that made a nice impression. However, this person did not have any proven leadership experience that could actually grow a church. If they actually call a new minister who is very much like the previous one, they will have a very happy congregation, but only for a short time until the demographic crisis results in the unsustainability of the church. The type of personality that the new minister should have would probably rub a lot of people the wrong way at first. An effective visionary and leader could, over time, bring the church back from the brink, and engage a whole new group of people and the community at large.

http://www.gods-business.com

This level of understanding individuals within our group provide us with the wisdom necessary to provide and encourage people where it is needed and to provide pushback when it is needed. Thereby we create a system of communication that allows us to say what needs to be said and hear what needs to be heard across the entire organization or team. Without it, team members can often end up talking past each other, or they perceive discord when really there should be none. In cases like this, the overall ministry of the church suffers because energy is taken from activities that should be performed and put into areas of conflict.

Background Checks

For both paid and volunteer staff, it is important to have personnel background checks. Frequently these are CORI background checks, although others may be used. These indicate if people have a felony background or not. Some volunteer organizations require higher levels of security, and, therefore, more stringent background checks may be conducted. Companies or organizations that provide insurance to our churches often require that these background checks be performed for liability purposes. Even if they do not have this kind of requirement, it is still a best practice that can help to keep our congregations, and especially our children, safe. No background check is foolproof, but it does reduce a church's risk exposure against fraud and violence. Some denominations have learned very painful lessons about the importance of background checks in terms of personnel safety after it was too late. It is easy to turn away and think our church or organization is immune to troubling behavior. The sad reality is that we should always be prepared for "when" this happens, instead of "if" this happens. Even if pastors themselves are not considered to be personally responsible for making sure these background checks are in place, as leaders of the church and CEOs of God's Business they have ultimate responsibility to make sure that all people and assets are safe and properly managed while on their watch.

> *I just couldn't believe it! Someone in the church had just told the congregation that a new person to our congregation liked to work on computers, and that if anyone was having computer problems at home, they should have this guy over to their house to fix it. The person making the announcement had no idea who this person really was. I had heard the guest tell some of his life story that he shared the week before, and decided to look up a particular incident that was mentioned online. There was no record of this person, of the tragedy described, or*

85

anything else. Yet here we were, telling some elderly people and single women to have their computer fixed at home by a complete stranger!

Many denominations have their own requirements about background checks and personnel procedures. Be sure to check with your denomination for their specific requirements.

There are a number of best practices for making sure the church members and property is safe. Often times when bad things happen, the people behind them have no previous criminal records. Therefore, we must minimize the risk and prevent opportunities for a first-time offender. To find out more about best practices in personnel management and property security see the free resources online or engage with experts in your community.

Team Management

Once churches reach a certain size, we have to have some level of staffing whether we pay for their work or not. Regardless whether they work for a check or on a volunteer basis, we need to treat them as professionals and have clear expectations of them and ways to accurately measure their success.

Many of us did not come into our positions with the goal of managing a staff. Some managerial elements may seem second nature to us, while some other issues can cost us a lot of time and anxiety. The following sections will provide some useful insights on how to handle a variety of situations, and will provide some tools so that you can be a really effective manager of other people. An important thing to remember is to always apply the golden rule. To do that well, we need to really understand other people and how they think. Then we can truly help all of those who are active in our ministry to flourish.

Professional Development

When we have both paid and unpaid members on a team, we may be inclined to treat them differently. From a personnel management standpoint however, we really should be blind to the fact that they do or do not receive payment in the form of currency. What's important from a managerial standpoint is to have intentional communications and to help them thrive in their role, which in turn will provide consistent energy, focus, and innovation to the entire ministry.

For many years, regular business practice has been to perform an annual employee review. In many cases, the employee is responsible for filling out at least half of the observation. It is not uncommon that managers who are not directly familiar with the employee actually complete the corporate side of the evaluation. Fortunately, top industry leaders are beginning to realize that this process is a waste of time. If we are to be effective managers, then we need frequent communication with the team member, and consistent focus on the vision and mission of the organization. We should also expect mutual feedback so that as managers we are not only providing feedback, but we are receiving it from our team as well. Keep in mind that negative feedback is not necessarily a bad thing. In fact, when it is used constructively, it benefits the team, the manager, and the entire organization.

> *I really enjoy what I do in terms of ministry and worship at the church. There are some really nice folks who frequently complement my work and the results that they see. Although I appreciate this, and I know they are being genuine, it would sometimes be helpful to have someone be more of a coach like I've had in other activities in the past. I know when I do something well, and I usually know when I don't. What I really am looking for is at least a peer or perhaps a mentor who can share meaningful (not always glowing) observations, and to*

provide possible solutions for how I can become even better at what I do. Coming from a trusted source, constructive criticism would give me more joy than blind praise.

If a church leader is hiring a new team member or managing an existing one, there needs to be clearly-stated objectives in a written document. This document will include the benchmarks for success, including measureable outcomes that are expected throughout the term of the position. All too often we have seen churches fail in staff retention and development because there have been no clear expectations for the role; people in leadership roles, the congregation, and even the employee all had different opinions about what a particular staff member should be doing and how they should be evaluated.

Employee manuals can be tedious, to say the least, but when created and revised on a regular basis, they can actually nurture exciting conversations and deeper relationships on ministerial teams. For example, the position description for an organist in the 1980s that continues to be reused today doesn't really address the needs that many of our churches have at the moment if the instruments have changed, the style of music has changed, the number of services has changed, and so forth. Instead, we need to start with the vision of the entire church and look at how the position of organist helps to achieve that mission. We should also consider the personal objectives of the organist at determine if he or she has a shared vision with the church. The same goes for virtually every position in the church from Senior Pastor to Custodian.

Hiring Practices

Attracting the best people for our ministry team can be very challenging, especially when most of our churches are not in a position to offer vast sums of money or prestige. Fortunately, the best recruits for our churches are not seeking these things anyway. So the question is how do we promote our positions and attract the right people? Usually the worst thing we can do is to try and hire a staff member away from another local church. As author Jim Muehlhausen states in his book, *The 51 Fatal Business Errors and How to Avoid Them*, hiring staff from your competitors is rarely a win. The most highly valued employees would be retained at all costs if they were really that good. So we have to ask: If another organization is willing to let a key employee leave without making him or her all sorts of counteroffers, then is that person someone that we really want to hire? This type of activity happens all the time in almost every industry, and the results are almost always the same. (Your situation may be different, but don't count on it.)

Therefore, the best way to attract the right people is to look beyond the specific skill set and a specific geographic area, and find the right personality type to fit in with the team. Within reason, specific skills can be developed and refined over time, but personality types cannot be easily changed. In the words of one highly successful business owner, "I can teach anyone the skills required to succeed in my organization, but I can't teach them to be nice."

Attracting the right person also means that we must have a willingness to challenge ourselves. We must absolutely correlate the personalities of the staff member to the objectives of the church to move the church in a specific direction. Obviously, the church is not usually in a position to teach new skills from scratch; candidates for a position should meet at least some basic criteria. But the successful hire can likely come from a place that is not initially expected, and also may help bring the church to places that hadn't been specifically envisioned.

It is important to note that when our church is advertising or publicizing an available position, the description must be entirely accurate and does not mislead in any way. This is especially true in terms of real expectations and compensation. Anything less than honesty is unethical. Our hiring team must also understand that, in our current state of need, a potential employee may have more power in negotiations than he or she realizes. To attract the right person, a congregation must be willing to communicate with them in that person's preferred manner right from the start. For example, a recent posting for a paid ministerial position community neglected to mention a salary range, any budget responsibility, or reporting structure. It also insisted that nobody should email or call the church with questions about the job. The only way to be considered for the position was to submit a resume online. Further exploration of that church's website did not provide any compelling reason why someone would want to work there. I suspect they will have big problems filling this position for quite some time, and that they will end up hiring a "compromise" candidate.

When was the last time you applied for a position? What was important for you to know about the job when you considered applying? Those are the things that church leaders must clearly state right from the start. If not, our relationship with the new employee will not begin with any high level of trust or mutual respect.

When searching for a new paid or volunteer staff member, the pastor or leadership team should have the resume evaluation process clearly defined even before the job is posted. In addition to the resume evaluation process, those responsible for making the hire need a clearly-stated interview (and audition) process. Usually the best practice is to have one point of contact with the applicants so that there will be a reduced likelihood that communication will be delayed or that conflicting messages will be sent out. The communication process should be seamless regardless of the size of the team conducting the search and making the hire. In some denominations, the pastor may have complete hire/fire authority. In most, there will be a team of people responsible for employee acquisition and development. Although this team may be in place, the pastor (or CEO of God's Business) must still accept ultimate responsibility in insuring the process is smooth and seamless. Otherwise the quality of the overall ministry could be jeopardized.

Staff Evaluations

We previously mentioned that annual staff evaluations are not generally effective. A better way to assess areas of success and places where improvements could be made is by having regular communication between a manager and a team member. These conversations are preferably conducted in person and in relatively informal dialogue. Annual reviews can only provide direction and encouragement once a year, but frequent conversations prevent either the manager or the team member from straying too far from the vision or current objectives.

Having frequent in-person conversations and then providing some documentation of the conversation to both the church and the team member more than satisfies the requirements of any reasonable human resources organization.

Staff evaluations are sometimes conducted within a team setting. If this is the case at your church, it is important that you or the designated team leader who leads the conversation ensures that it does not become personal in nature and that criticisms do not become attacks. The manager should also ensure that compliments do not become merely blanket praise. None of these are useful to the team member or the church. Remember that if reviews are done in a team format, all individuals should have the opportunity to reflect on the team as whole as well as the individual contributors. It is important that these team reviews include paid and volunteer staff alike. Volunteers should have frequent individual reviews as well.

Non-profit organizations, and especially churches, frequently take the view that if someone is giving freely of their time, then a manager cannot thoughtfully criticize or perhaps even reprimand a staff member even if it is truly warranted. Nothing could be further from the truth. Volunteers, like paid staff, are the face of our church to the congregation and the community at large.

We simply cannot risk our congregation or God's Business when someone does something that puts the organization in jeopardy or tarnishes its reputation. The litmus test for everyone is that they share the mission and vision of the church above their own personal aspirations in their role.

This brings us to the discussion of unfortunate situations that sometimes occur at church. Sometimes volunteers and paid staff are no longer suited for current or future ministries in the church either because of a lack of skills, a poor personality fit, or a loss of commitment. In such cases we may need to accept the fact that the best solution is to terminate the team member. Termination should never be used as a judgment against a person, and it can only be seen as a mutual failure for failing to keep the employee engaged with the change in organization vision and mission. Nevertheless, it is sometimes the only appropriate response to the situation or church's changing requirements. When we get to the point of firing a staff member, it is necessary to do it as quickly, as lovingly, and as equitably as possible.

Staff Development

As previously stated, our churches ideally attract people who are not looking for fame and fortune. The best paid and volunteer staff is generally rewarded in ways (other than or in addition to money) that are meaningful to

95

them. This may be the ability to acquire new skills, refine skills they already have, try out new ministries, engage with different people, and to receive deeper forms of spiritual and cognitive encouragement. As such, one of the best ways to continue to engage and develop staff members is to provide them with opportunities for personal and professional development, including offering sabbaticals.

If your church is part of a large denomination, then you probably already have a number of opportunities for your staff to participate in professional and personal development activities that can address these needs. There are also a number of online resources that can provide some of these same things, and they may prove to be equally effective in some situations. Staff members at all levels can benefit from these types of opportunities which will inspire them and encourage them to grow in new directions. It doesn't matter their position is janitorial, educational, or pastoral. The only way to know which type of program would be most beneficial to your staff member is to ask him or her directly. Professional development opportunities would take place at least once a year if appropriate, but they can be more or less frequent depending upon the circumstances. Remember that most of our staff members will either be employed somewhere else in addition to their church position, or they may be retired or engaged in other activities besides the church. Most people who are not permanent, full-time employees of the church are not in a position to commit 100% of their time to the church. We should not expect them to. Therefore, personal and professional development opportunities should be offered but not required, lest they become an undue burden on our staff and provide no real benefit.

Employee/Church Manuals

For church employees, volunteer staff, and the congregation itself, we must have written documentation of mutual expectations and measures of success for the organization. Employee manuals should expand upon the details that are outlined in any job description, and they should help the employee understand *how* these objectives can be met, rather than just *what* objectives should be met. Employee manuals should clearly define processes and procedures for routine and ad hoc activities. Any ambiguity in our employee manuals opens up the possibility for future misunderstanding and conflict. Although it is impossible to have a perfect church manual, we should make every effort to have clear documentation that is agreed upon by everyone. Church manuals should include guidelines not only for employees but also for church operations and procedures, including church meeting guidelines.

Expectations of the congregation and its individual members need to be stated as well.

> *We had a member of the congregation show up at one of our leadership meetings. In our church, any member may attend these meetings, but if they want to say anything, they need to have requested to do so ahead of time, and it needs to be put on the agenda. This has usually worked pretty well at keeping meetings productive and not running overly late. At this particular meeting, this individual interrupted the process and demanded that one of the ministerial team members be terminated. This did not have anything to do with anything illegal, it was nothing that was a morality issue or anything else, he simply wanted this person to be removed because he didn't see the minister as being effective.*
>
> *Nobody on the leadership team stopped him from continuing the rant. The pastor did not take control of the situation. Nobody seemed to have an idea of what to do in this situation. If we had a mutual agreement about how meetings would be run AND we*

98

had been willing to enforce those rules, then this situation could have been stopped much earlier. Instead what we got was a lot a pent-up anger, embarrassment, and hurt feelings. In our denomination, the pastor is the ultimate authority at the local church level. Unfortunately, the pastor was not prepared on how to handle the situation, and the church had no clear document about how an issue like this should be addressed. Even after this happened, we have not made any real effort to provide written guidance to the congregation and staff. We can only hope that it doesn't happen again on our watch.

It is reasonable to assume that smaller churches may not have this level of documentation. And if you are in the process of starting your own church from scratch, this is not where you should put your energy. However, those who are leading churches that have any staff (paid or not) besides the pastor should have a reasonable level of documentation. You can basically guarantee that, without it, you will encounter conflict that will not be easily resolved and that can cause long-term damage.

Regarding Leadership Teams

For those of us in churches that have a team of people in leadership positions, we should be intentional about how well the demographics of the team reflects the demographics of our congregation and, ideally, the demographics of the community in which we serve. In too many cases, the leadership team in small churches may not represent the current reality or the desired direction of the community. Perhaps the leadership team is made up of mostly retired people while other church members who are actively working, parenting, or volunteering in outside organizations are not active in church leadership because of scheduling conflicts or unreasonable expectations. It is not always possible to have leadership teams that actively reflect the overall demographics of the church and the community. In order for our ministry to be successful in the long term, however, this is something we absolutely need to strive for.

Importance of Mentoring Others and Being Coached

A final note on professional development is the opportunity for pastors and other trusted leaders to mentor and coach our paid and volunteer staff. It is one of the greatest gifts that we have to offer our team.

When we consider that Jesus himself showed and encouraged people along the right path, it is easy to see how important it is that we do the same for others. On the other hand, it is just as important to allow others to coach and mentor us.

Coaching programs for leaders of almost any kind are readily available. They can be in-person or online, and they usually provide substantial value and reward in terms of personal and ministerial transformation. Some people may consider asking for help or advice to be a sign of weakness or conceding our authority to someone else. Deep down we know that becoming our best selves only happens when we work with and for others. We owe it to our staff to help them become the best that they can be in their ministry. We also owe it to our staff, to ourselves, and to our congregation to become the best pastors and leaders that we can be. The most successful people in the world usually have someone guiding them along the way and cheering them on in the process. You deserve that too!

In Summary

None of the topics in this chapter overrides the vision and mission of the church. By keeping clear expectations and proper communication channels open, we can be more effective as a whole since we will spend less energy on conflict, and more on transformation. There are a number of free resources available to you online. Also, consider getting involved with a "mastermind" group, or engaging with a coach for a while. These things can help you to thrive in your ministry, and recharge you in the event that you have become a little frustrated or fatigued.

Chapter 6: Accounting & Finance

And the Lord said, "Who then is the faithful and prudent manager whom his master will put in charge of his slaves, to give them their allowance of food at the proper time? Blessed is that slave whom his master will find at work when he arrives. Truly I tell you, he will put that one in charge of all his possessions. But if that slave says to himself, 'My master is delayed in coming,' and if he begins to beat the other slaves, men and women, and to eat and drink and get drunk, the master of that slave will come on a day when he does not expect him and at an hour that he does not know, and will cut him off, and put him with the unfaithful. That slave who knew what his master wanted, but did not prepare himself or do what was wanted, will receive a severe beating. But the one who did not know and did what deserved a beating will receive a light beating. From everyone to whom much has been given, much will be required; and from the one to whom much has been entrusted, even more will be demanded."

– Luke 12:42-48

Chapter Overview

Money is probably one of the biggest topics pertaining to operating a small church (and I suspect many large ones as well). We have all heard the saying, "No money, no mission." The balancing act that we face as church leaders is to be trusted stewards with God's money, yet not to become obsessed with it. A wise pastor friend once said that, "God doesn't need one penny of your money." (This was rather a bombshell during pledge time!) This is true, but our ministries and ministers need to have some level of income in order to stay in existence.

This chapter is not intended to go into great detail about accounting practices and tax classifications. As I tell my wife during tax season, "There are people for that." However, as church leaders we absolutely must be proficient in understanding the "why" behind accounting practices rather than the "how." Ideally, we have people outside of our congregations handling our bookkeeping and governmental filings. The truth is that most smaller churches rely on volunteers or staff who are not trained, let alone bonded. In either case, many pastors are serving as the "CEO" of the local church. As such, he or she must understand what financial statements mean at face value, their implication the future, and what to focus on first when trouble is around the corner.

As always, pastors and church leaders should eagerly engage with external resources who are trusted and certified in their field. Having an outside bookkeeper and accountant (as well as legal representation) can actually save a lot of internal stress and minimize exposure to conflict or even legal actions by not having amateurs do the job of professionals. You and your organization will also be able to devote more time and energy to ministry rather than management.

A number of free resources are available to you online. Check your denominational leadership and local Chambers of Commerce for outside resources that can assist you and your leadership team in this sometimes tricky topic.

Cash Management

14 "For it will be like a man going on a journey, who called his servants and *entrusted to them his property. ¹⁵ To one he* *gave five talents, to another two, to another* *one, to each according to his ability. Then* *he went away. ¹⁶ He who had received the* *five talents went at once and traded with* *them, and he made five talents more. ¹⁷ So* *also he who had the two talents made two* *talents more. ¹⁸ But he who had received the* *one talent went and dug in the ground and* *hid his master's money.¹⁹ Now after a long* *time the master of those servants came* *and settled accounts with them. ²⁰ And he* *who had received the five talents came* *forward, bringing five talents more, saying,* *'Master, you delivered to me five talents;* *here I have made five talents more.' ²¹ His* *master said to him, 'Well done, good* *and faithful servant. You have been faithful* *over a little; I will set you over much. Enter* *into the joy of your master.'²² And he also* *who had the two talents came forward,* *saying, 'Master, you delivered to me two* *talents; here I have made two talents* *more.'²³ His master said to him, 'Well done,* *good and faithful servant. You have been* *faithful over a little; I will set you over* *much. Enter into the joy of your* *master.' [24] He also who had received the one talent came forward, saying, 'Master, I knew you to be a hard man, reaping where you did not sow, and gathering where you scattered no seed, [25] so I was afraid, and I went and hid your talent in the ground. Here you have what is yours.' [26] But his master answered him, 'You wicked and slothful servant! You knew that I reap where I have not sown and gather where I scattered no seed? [27] Then you ought to have invested my money with the bankers, and at my coming I should have received what was my own with interest. [28] So take the talent from him and give it to him who has the ten talents. [29] For to everyone who has will more be given, and he will have an abundance. But from the one who has not, even what he has will be taken away. [30] And cast the worthless servant into the outer darkness. In that place there will be weeping and gnashing of teeth.' – Matthew 25: 14-30*

The ability to manage cash is the most important skill for a small business to have. Pastors and church leaders need to have the same skills if they want their local churches to thrive. When cash flow becomes an issue, the usual reaction is to take our eye off the ball and focus on money instead of mission when, in fact, a healthy church always does both.

Without suitable cash or access to funds (liquid assets), churches can find themselves in a position of being unable to sustain important programs or create new ones. Evangelism and mission are often sacrifices for building maintenance and salaries during cash crunches. And there is often a prevailing feeing of dread with some leaders, and an annoyance by the congregation by hearing about how they need to contribute more.

Cash management, therefore, is a key element for a successful ministry at any level. The best tool to manage cash is by using a cash forecast report, sometimes called "Cash Projections". This helps leaders recognize what an organization's cash flow is going to be in the future, and identifies financial glitches or challenges. With this information, leaders can be proactive in managing cash and avoiding these problems.

In small congregations, money comes into the church from direct contributions from the members. There are usually other community fundraisers, but a bulk of the money comes in the form of pledges and directed giving. In this case, established churches usually have a pretty good idea about how much will come in and when. Obviously external factors can greatly impact budget projections, but, in general, the leaders have a reasonable set of financial expectations based on history. Looking at history and combining it with experience and analysis, periods of negative cash flows (more money is going out than coming in) can be anticipated and addressed. It is not unusual for these peaks and valleys in cash flow to be cyclical in nature, usually in relation to church holidays and summer vacations.

A best practice for small business is to do rolling thirteen (13)-week forecasts of cash. This means that, from any given point in time, the organization has expectations for the cash situation for the next quarter. This rolling forecast is then compared to the plan that you actually thought was going to happen (Budget), and then you can make adjustments as the organization goes forward. If this is done on a weekly basis, it is easier to avoid pitfalls that are coming down the road by adjusting discretionary payments ahead of time. Fixed payments (like salaries, utilities, other fees) cannot be easily adjusted and come in on a schedule. Therefore, our discretionary spending is the only thing we can quickly change. We can, of course, try to increase revenue, but that is usually harder to do, especially in times when projected revenue is already less than projected expense.

Budgets

A budget is just a document; it doesn't actually control anything. We have fixes expenses like salaries and so forth that you can kind of estimate. But things like utility bills, heating oil and snow plowing are a lot harder to estimate. Last year we put in $3,000 for snow plowing. Because of the record snowfall, we ended up spending between $8,000 and $10,000 just for snow removal.

So we could do one of two things: we could go back to the congregations and say, "So here we are, folks. You know we're spending an extra $7,000 to plow the parking lot, so you need to dig into your pockets a little deeper, or you will have to be digging snow instead." The only other options are to try to borrow money or to take money out of endowments. No matter how well you plan, you can still be broadsided by unexpected events.

Many churches (and small businesses) operate off the seat of their pants. They often do not have a realistic (or any) budget in place. A budget is a financial plan which helps an organization to conduct cash flow forecasting. Budgets look at the plan for spending money for the

110

church over the course of a year, broken down monthly. Financial projections then look at how much money is expected to come in to the church and provide a comparison of income versus expense, usually on a monthly and annual written statement (Balance Sheet).

A big question is why doesn't every organization have a budget? Without a budget, it is impossible to know what the real plan is. Leaders may have a general idea of where they want to be, but they don't have a documented plan (budget) in place. Leaders without a plan should know their fate!

Balance Sheets

Balance sheets compare the budget to actual spending. They also provide an assessment of the cash and assets of the church. Created monthly and annually, balance sheets provide a historical picture of what has already happened financially. Like identifying a particular position of an atom, by the time you get the information, it has already moved.

Balance sheets tie into cash management as well. Usually, when you look at your balance sheet at the end of the year, you want to look at it side-by-side with the balance sheet from the previous year. For example, in January 2016, you would be looking at the current balance sheet along with the one for 2015 and even for 2014. When you look at the cash reported in these statements, you can see how it has been changing over time. As someone who understands finances, you want to look at what you actually have (assets) year over year.

The "quick ratio" is an easy tool to quickly compare the financial health of an organization to its position in previous years. This ratio is calculated by taking all current assets and dividing that amount by all current liabilities. This ratio is then compared to the ratio from previous years to see how the organization is trending from a financial standpoint.

Another think to look at are the accounts payable (AP). A key question to ask is how often are you paying your bills? Are you on time or are you late? Ideally, you want to be collecting money faster than you are paying your bills, which indicates that you have a positive cash flow.

Finally, churches may want to look at its revenue versus the number of church members or pledging units. (A pledging unity may be a family that gives one gift as a whole rather than each family member making a unique financial contribution.) Changes in the ratio of giving to pledging unit can be an effective "check engine light" for problematic trends into the future. For example, a church may have sufficient funding provided mostly by a few big donors. If something happens to one of the larger donors, it can put a lot of financial stress on the rest of the organization.

Controls

I have known pastors who have been in ministry 25 to 30 years. We have had management and leadership discussions and so forth, and they will say to me that they don't even want to know about the money because that will distract them. I tell them very strongly that even if you don't know who gives what, you'd better know how much the church brings in and where it goes. Otherwise you're shooting yourself in the foot!

In private industry, balance sheets and sometimes other financial statements can be easily manipulated. Public companies frequently report in ways that impact cash balance either higher or lower depending on what they are trying to accomplish in terms of stock prices or some other objective. Small organizations can do the same type of thing depending on the financial messages that they are trying to send.

As pastors and church leaders, we generally do not have goals of artificially manipulating financial statements. Our primary concern is keeping the organization healthy so that we can be effective in our ministry. The most effective way to prevent artificial manipulation of balance sheets, and also to protect against fraud conducted by employees or volunteers, is to have a system of financial controls in place.

Financial controls should be clearly documented, and they can be as simple as having a system to manage petty cash and for purchasing smaller items like office supplies. They may also include requiring two signatures on checks over a certain amount. Avoiding having any "corporate credit cards" is also a good idea. Finally, hiring outside accountants and auditors will make it much more difficult for an insider to steal any money. Churches (and all non-profit businesses) usually have a board that oversees the running of the organization. For the members and contributors to have a "warm, fuzzy feeling" about the church, they should want to know that financial statements are not being manipulated and that everything is above board. It's really in the best interest of our churches to have either an annual review or a full-blown audit by an external financial firm.

Avoiding Financial Pitfalls

The way that churches and small businesses deal with potential problems down the road is to be proactive. There are two issues with cash: the cash coming in (revenue) and the cash going out (expenses). If you see a potential problem arising (probably from a cash forecast report), you shouldn't focus on only one side of the fence. Both revenue and expenses should be examined.

Sometimes, organizations try to accelerate the amount of cash coming in to deal with a current difficulty or need. The problem is that there may be additional financial obligations coming down the road soon after that will not be able to be met. Some financial decisions are never easy (like reducing salaries and programs), but it is best to tackle them right away rather than waiting until it's too late.

Non-Profit Organizations

The U.S. tax code is something to behold. For the sake of this chapter, we will not be going deeply into 501(c)(3) and other tax-exempt organizations. However, if your church or ministry is not already registered as a 501(c)(3), then you may be missing out on some opportunities that could help you grow.

Besides tax exemption (which churches already have), this recognition can help you qualify to receive grants, lower your postal rates, and to provide tax deduction status for special ministries and programs. Even if you have this recognition, there are still annual filings that need to be made with federal and state agencies (or both). Check out the free resources online for more information, or contact a trusted tax expert in your community.

In Summary

There are three key takeaways from this chapter. If a small church pays close attention to these details and manages them effectively, then the money will not distract from the overall vision and mission of the church.

First, cash management is vital. We hear in the secular world that "cash is king." This is obviously incorrect from our theological perspective. However, whether we run a non-profit or a for-profit organization, there must be cash on hand, or access to funding and the ability to pay it back, otherwise the organization will fail.

Second, budgets are extremely important. These cannot be pie-in-the-sky budgets, but real estimates based on past performance of the church and intelligent analysis for the future. Since budgets are only a guide for how money will flow in and out of an organization, they do not reflect firm reality like a Statement of Cash Flows. That being said, churches must plan carefully for what income will be had (and when), and the priorities for how it will be spent. Budgets and Statements of Cash Flows are moral documents. If you want to know what is really important to your church, look at where the money goes.

Finally, internal controls are really important for churches, as they are for any organization. It should be as simple as possible to have documented controls in

116

place to monitor each financial transaction. The threat of fraud cannot be completely eliminated, but good controls can greatly reduce the possibility that financial fraud will ever happen in our churches.

Remember to check your denominational leadership and local resources that can help you sail smoothly thorough the stormy seas of finance.

Chapter 7: Property Management and Building Maintenance

"The condition and quality of (the church) buildings reflect (the congregation's) pride or indifference, the level of prosperity in the area, social values and behavior, and all the many influences both past and present, which combine to give a community its unique character."

(Paraphrased from Paul Lobsworth, Lee's Building Maintenance Management)

Chapter Overview

Most churches in America have a physical location that they call "home." This may be a stand-alone church building, a campus-style setup, a storefront in a shopping plaza, or even a mobile or modular home. Whether the building is owned, leased, or financed, it almost always

118

represents a congregation's largest asset. However, sometimes it also represents some of its biggest liabilities.

In addition to the structure itself, the major systems and equipment required to make the structures functional for worship and administration also represent significant investments. Heating and cooling systems (HVAC), electrical systems, plumbing, seating, altars, office equipment, sound equipment, organs, pianos, and a host of other components come with a staggering price tag for even modest churches.

Many of us may never experience serving in a church that has a completely new physical plant. So, to keep our facilities operational, we must understand how our facilities work and the best way to keep them working well. We also need to be comfortable and confident in our maintenance and repair planning systems as well as having a carefully documented system for hiring contractors and other personnel.

This chapter will highlight several areas of key importance to our churches. It will also provide a thorough checklist for maintenance programs, sample items for your policy and procedure manual, and some useful insights and experiences from real-world pastors and leaders.

Building Maintenance

You can't overestimate the impact that property management has on a congregation. Even modest churches usually have complex physical plant systems, which incorporate electrical systems, information technology and communications, plumbing, HVAC, plus various security and alarm systems. All of this is in addition to maintaining the buildings and grounds themselves.

The fact is, when most of us think of church, an image of a physical location and campus usually comes to mind. Regardless of where a congregation is on the theological scale, its identity is closely tied to the location where people come together to worship, pray, and to learn. Our church buildings should provide us with a functional and safe place to assemble, while also helping us receive the inspiration and support that we need to go back out into the world.

As pastors and church leaders, we must ensure that our facilities serve our congregations and community well, both in the present and into the future. To do that, we must have thorough inventories of our property along with reasonable action plans and checklists for its maintenance and replacement.

Understanding Your Building Needs

Most of us serve a congregation that already has a building or campus. The sites and buildings were selected to meet a specific congregational need or vision at that particular time. Over the years, however, congregations change and the buildings may no longer be ideally suited for the current realities. We should shy away from continually asking ourselves whether or not our physical plant should be maintained, modified, or even replaced.

The first step is to ask ourselves one question: can we achieve the level of utility that we need from our existing physical plant in its current condition, or do we need to make changes? If a change is necessary, then we need to decide if we should increase or decrease the size of our physical plant. From there, we need to determine what expenses are reasonable to realize the needed changes.

Expenses must be weighed against the actual value that the physical plant provides to the congregation's vision and mission. When the expense of the property is out of sync with the vision and mission, alternate plans need to be considered for long-term viability of the congregation. To judge whether expenses are reasonable or not, consider these four factors:

- Is the amount and quality of the work done consistent with the expense? Consider prevailing labor rates, cost of materials, and time to completion. Is the amount and quality of the work performed in line with what can be provided by other suppliers?
- Is the work performed necessary for safety and security? Can it be avoided by using other reasonable methods? If the work is not performed, will it impact the amount or quality of services offered by the church, will it compromise safety and security in any way, will the church be in violation of any city safety codes?
- Can the church thrive without the work being performed? Is the work needed in order to expand the current mission or to prepare for imminent growth and the future vision of the church?
- Is the congregation going to be at risk because of the financial expense? Can the existing congregation cover the costs through promised giving and existing church funds? Are there external sources of funding or guarantees that will minimize the financial risk?

If these questions are difficult to answer, then we should take a step back and ask ourselves one question: can we achieve the level of utility that we need from our existing physical plant in its current condition, or do we need to make changes? If a change is necessary, then we need to decide if we should increase or decrease the size of our physical plant. From there, we can refer back to the four questions above to determine what expenses are reasonable.

Our church is building a third floor onto one of the wings of the existing building. We have an ongoing relationship with a variety of non-profits who all rent space from us. So we've decided to be intentional about these relationships and to build a non-profit community center. There are now offices that are staffed throughout the week by different non-profit groups who rent space from us. One of these groups places non-profit professionals in the field. Another is a youth chorus. These and other groups all benefit from the non-profit center created by the church, and the church has benefitted greatly from having them share our space.

Asset Planning and Facilities Management

A systematic approach to asset planning allows your church to make thoughtful and informed decisions about property maintenance and management. Having a plan in place prevents hurried and stressful conversations that can come about when unanticipated things happen to a building or equipment. Ideally, having a detailed plan will avoid the unexpected almost entirely since you will know our current inventory, its condition, and contingency plan.

Ideally, an architect or designer would provide a maintenance manual for the building and its major components. This would detail the life cycle of the building itself, major systems like HVAC, as well as projected energy requirements. In most cases, your church many not have any such original documentation. In this case, you should perform cost analyses in order to understand the current conditions and use of the church buildings. Resources can then be effectively allocated in order to maintain, refurbish, or rebuild the physical plant.

Property Inventory

It is easy to assemble a detailed property inventory of new buildings by using final drawings and invoices, which identify the major components and contents. Older buildings will require on-site inspections to identify the major building components and contents as well as their current condition.

The property inventory should contain the following items (more may be added depending of your specific situation):

- The physical location of the property – this may be the street address or a more specific mapping based on county survey documents
- The age of the structure and each major component
- A description of how the property is currently used, and any anticipated changes in future usage
- Size of the building – including number of stories, square footage, and total area under a roof
- Construction materials
- Utilities and communication services that enter the building
- Projected remaining useful life of each structure and service
- Occupation costs
- Replacement cost
- Property (site) value

125

- Zoning considerations
- Other factors such as threats due to severe weather, proximity to major transportation routes, and social instability in the area

To determine the condition of the building and its major components for your property inventory, a physical inspection will be required. Special attention should be given to elements that are critical to the operations of the church. Items at the greatest risk of failure should also be carefully noted. Besides the building itself, major components include:

- HVAC
- Stained Glass and other decorative components of the building(s)
- Electrical Systems
- Plumbing
- Network / Communications (Computer / IT)
- Lighting
- Security Systems
- Sound / Video Systems
- Organs and Pianos
- Carpeting and Flooring
- Pews / Congregation Seating
- Altars and Liturgical Apparatus
- Statuary and Artwork

- Parking Lots
- Steeple
- Playgrounds
- Signs

Rather than trying to describe verbally the condition of every element, it will be easier for your church to create a standardized grading system. This will allow you to record the condition of the building and its components more consistently, especially if multiple people will be performing the assessment. We suggest using a five-tier grading system:

A = New / Like-new (fully functional and no signs of wear)

B = Good (fully functional, some signs of wear)

C = Fair (mostly operational but some impairment, moderate wear)

D = Poor (function significantly impaired, significant wear)

E = Needs Replacement (excessive wear, nonfunctional or dangerous)

An itemized property condition worksheet is available to you online at www.gods-business.com/resources. This will help you create a thorough inventory and condition assessment, including maintenance and replacement cost estimates.

Your organization should have an action plan for the maintenance, refurbishment, and replacement for the physical plant and the major components. Whether you own or lease your property, you will be responsible for creating a reasonable plan as well as making sure you have the financial resources needed to manage your buildings and the major components according to that plan.

Often times a church will have to make tough decisions about which maintenance projects to pursue and which projects to postpone due to financial or other constraints. In order to establish your particular maintenance priorities, consider which building spaces and components are under-utilized or perhaps not used at all. If a significant expenditure is required for the maintenance or refurbishment of a component, it must be justified by some sort of return on investment (ROI). ROI may take the form of a financial return, increased safety or comfort, greater efficiency, or some other benefit (such as the ability to offer an important new service to the congregation or community). Without a quantifiable ROI, these projects should not be undertaken.

Accessibility / Universal Design

President George H.W. Bush signed the Americans with Disabilities Act (ADA) into law in 1990. Although your church may not be responsible for meeting its specific guidelines (most states do not require churches to follow the guidelines), it provides a clear benchmark for buildings and property to be accessible to everyone with physical disabilities or mental impairment.

> *18 Some men took a man who was not able to move his body to Jesus. He was carried on a bed. They looked for a way to take the man into the house where Jesus was. 19 But they could not find a way to take him in because of so many people. They made a hole in the roof over where Jesus stood. Then they let the bed with the sick man on it down before Jesus. 20 When Jesus saw their faith, He said to the man, "Friend, your sins are forgiven."*

- *Luke 5:18-20*

We will not go into any great detail about the ADA other than to mention that its guidelines represent elements that our buildings should incorporate, if at all possible, in order for us to be able to welcome members and guests into our midst. It may not always be practical to have a handicap entrance at the main doors of a historic church, for example. It nevertheless sends a signal to a person in a wheelchair that, because she must use a separate entrance, sit in a specific place, or seek help to open doors, use the facilities, and so forth, she may not be as valued as those who can use the front door.

Some key accessibility and safety measures to keep in mind include:

- Accessible routes and entrances/exits
- Parking spaces and passenger loading zones
- Stairways, ramps, and elevators
- Restrooms (including family and assisted restrooms)
- Fire alarms
- Signs
- Assistive listening and other communication systems
- Dining and work surfaces
- Kitchen areas
- Floor and ground surfaces
- Turning area for wheelchairs and scooters
- Protruding objects
- Light switches and automatic lighting

- Doors, hallways, and gates
- Automatic door openers
- Handrails

When building or updating your church campus, the principles of universal design (broad-spectrum ideas meant to produce buildings, products, and environments that are inherently accessible to older people, people without disabilities, and people with disabilities) will help you to create an outward sign of your welcome to all people, and will provide a safe and useful space for generations to come. For more information, visit www.ada.gov or www.universaldesign.com.

My husband and I were going to a funeral out of state. Although we managed to make it to the building just in time, we could not actually get into the sanctuary before the funeral started. Unfortunately, there were only a couple handicap spaces in the parking lot, and they were long gone, so we had to park far away in order to find a place big enough to deploy the ramp of our van. When we got to the church building, there was no sign for a handicap entrance, even though there was an elevator. The elevator unfortunately opened up directly in the front of the sanctuary. When we went in, all eyes were on us. How embarrassing!

Selecting Contractors

When your church needs updates or modifications to the buildings or equipment, it is important to find people who are truly experts in their field and who will charge a fair (although not necessarily the lowest) price for their work.

It is all too common to hear stories of churches that had a few "do-it-yourselfers" in the congregation and ended up with sometimes disastrous results – broken equipment, projects completed incorrectly, and a lot of hurt feelings.

Our church used to have a beautiful Weber grand piano. It had been selected especially for the church by a concert pianist affiliated with the congregation. It was originally located in a large performance space on the second floor, but the new music director wanted it moved to the choir room on the first floor. Keep in mind that the church is a historic structure, and has no elevator. A group of men from the church thought they could move the piano themselves after Sunday services. Unfortunately, by the time the piano had slid out of control down to the first floor, there was nothing left of it to play. The staircase and wall was badly damaged too. At least nobody got hurt (too badly).

Here are some tips for identifying and hiring the right people for major construction or specialty jobs at your church:

Recommendations

Using your contacts in and out of the church, ask around for recommendations of people who may be able to do your project. You may also check national associations, your local chamber of commerce, your denominational office, and other local clergy and business owners for names of qualified professionals. Building inspectors and licensing boards may also be a valuable resource for referrals, recommendations, and lists of professionals.

Phone Interviews

Make a quick call to all of the prospects on your list. If they do not answer, see how long it takes for them to return your call. Some sample questions for you to ask are:

- Do they take on projects like yours?
- Will they provide references?
- Are they licensed, insured, and bonded?
- How many projects do they work on at the same time?

- Do they use their own labor, or do they hire subcontractors?
- Who serves as their project manager?

How they answer these questions will give you a clue as to the company's reliability, how much they will be focused on your project, and how smoothly the project may go.

In-person Meeting

Once you have completed your phone interviews, select your top candidates and schedule an in-person meeting with each of them. Ideally, they will come to your location so they can learn more about the project first-hand. It is important that you communicate well together; otherwise there could be problems during the project. Also, the most refined sales presentation does not necessarily indicate the best work. Follow your instincts, but also check sources like the Better Business Bureau, Angie's List, Yelp, and others to see if there have been any disputes or complaints. Note that it is not uncommon for good businesses to receive a complaint or two over time. Some people are extremely difficult to please and have unreasonable expectations. However, a pattern of unsatisfied customers or similar complaints may indicate that a company isn't right for you.

Check References and Results

134

Call the references provided by the company to confirm their satisfaction with the project. Ask about the successful completion of the project. Was it on time and on budget? You may also want to visit a current job site, if possible, to observe the operation. Look for work habits that are neat and safe. Also look for laborers who are respectful of the owner's property.

Get Bids

Once you have your "short-list" of contractors, invite them to submit bids for your project. The contractors may need to see specific plans or written requirements, and they may also have a list of questions for you pertaining to your specific project and the current state of your building and its systems.

Ask that the bids be submitted in writing, and that the cost of materials, labor, and other expenses are itemized. Also make sure that the timeline is clearly determined. This way, you will have an easier time comparing the bids that you receive.

It is generally wiser to receive a fixed cost bid, meaning that the church does not pay for any additional hours. Whereas consultants, lawyers, and other business services may charge by the hour, structural and mechanical projects should be paid according to the successful completion of the project, not the amount of time that it took to complete.

Make sure that the process to make changes is clearly written into the bid. Should something unforeseen happen, both you and the contractor need to have an agreement how changes will be made and compensated.

Set a Payment Schedule

The payment schedule for a project may tell you a bit about a contractor's work ethic and financial situation. Beware of a request for too high of a percentage up front. This may indicate a lack of trust or some cash flow issues. Most contracts require a small percentage (around 10%) when a contract is signed. Subsequent payments are made upon the completion of set milestones of the project, with the final payment being due upon completion of the entire project. It is important that your church keeps its end of the agreement. Never keep a contractor waiting for payment when it is due. This could cause problems for your project and also sully your reputation as a church.

Price

The most important factor in selecting a contractor is your level of trust (based on your research) and the quality of your mutual communication. It is also a good practice to throw out any "lowball" bids since it may mean that the contractor cuts corners or worse. Successful contractors should all provide bids that are reasonably close to each other.

Put Everything in Writing

Make sure that your contract clearly describes every phase of the project, the payment schedule, proof of insurance (liability and worker's compensation), a fixed schedule, an itemized materials list, and lien releases (in the case of large equipment being installed that the contractor does not pay for). Once again, make sure that the process to introduce any changes into the planned project is clearly defined and that there is no ambiguity regarding the cost of these changes.

Thorough contracts are written artifacts of mutual trust. Just as the old saying goes, "Good fences make good neighbors," so too, do "Clear contracts make happy partners."

We have a person in our congregation whose family owns a roofing company. A number of years ago, the church went out to bid because they needed some roof repairs done. Her family's company did not come in with the lowest bid. There was a lot of consternation and a lot of tension because they are members of the congregation, and

137

they also pledge faithfully. Years later, there are still hurt feelings. Fortunately, they did not leave the church though.

Property and Liability Insurance

In today's world of risk of loss and litigation, your church should carry sufficient property and liability insurance. If your church is part of a larger denomination, check to see what denominational requirements may be in place and if there is a preferred insurance provider. Be sure to seek out a professional who can help you and your leadership team make the best choices of providers and coverage rates.

Property Insurance

This type of insurance protects your church against damage or destruction due to negligence, natural disasters, and faulty structures and systems. Property insurance may also protect you against theft and vandalism. Check your coverage carefully to see what exemptions in coverage may exist, especially if you are in known high-risk areas.

In some cases, it is worth considering extra endorsements (a change to an insurance policy that adds

to or restricts the original coverage terms). Types of
endorsements include:

- Guarding against inflation – automatic
adjustments for property and content valuation
- Bonds – paying for loss resulting from theft or
other dishonest activity of personnel
- Equipment malfunction – covers losses resulting
from the breakdown of key equipment

Liability Insurance

Liability insurance protects the church finances and
church staff against claims of injury or property damage.
This kind of insurance was created specifically to protect
institutions and individuals against third-party lawsuits or
insurance claims. Personal injury and property damaged
caused willfully or by negligence is usually not covered
by liability insurance.

Check your specific policy to see if how your
insurance carrier treats legal costs. They may or may not
impact your policy limits.

Besides the basic coverage for injury and property
damage, enhanced coverage is usually available for
specialized injury (such as emotional injury), teacher
liability, and leadership team liability. Sadly, the events of
recent years have also created the need for other

enhanced liability protection like sexual acts liability, counseling liability, and computer-related liability.

Umbrella Policies (Excess Liability Insurance)

Unfortunately, our churches and ministries are not immune to legal action from inside or outside of the organization. In recent years, we have seen that negligence by clergy, churches, and entire denominations has resulted in multi-million dollar lawsuits. In the event that your church is subject to litigation and the damages exceed your basic liability coverage, an umbrella policy can protect your assets that would otherwise be at risk.

Selecting Insurance Providers

Before selecting an insurance representative for your church or organization, it is important to understand the difference between Agents and Brokers.

Insurance agents represent one or more specific insurance companies, and they sell policies only for the company or companies that they represent. Insurance agents are paid commissions based on their sales of insurance.

Brokers are people that work for you specifically. They are not appointed or employed by insurance companies. Brokers are hired to keep their eye on the

140

market and to provide you with the best options at any given time. It may be advantageous to use a broker instead of an agent if you want the assurance of having competitive pricing across the industry rather than a smaller selection of companies. Brokers are also paid by commission on their sales, but they must disclose their fees to their clients.

To select an agent or broker, the process is not unlike that for hiring a contractor although it should be less complicated. The best place to start is to see if your denomination has any established relationships with insurance providers. In some cases, you may get insurance through your denomination itself.

If your denomination does not have established insurance plans or connections, then you should consider getting referrals from your local church leaders, other pastors, the Chamber of Commerce, or other sources. It is also a good idea to check Angie's List or other customer review sites for information pertaining to the quality of service provided by the insurance carrier, agent, and/or broker.

One word of caution: if you are considering purchasing insurance online, make sure that the policy will provide you with the coverage that you actually need. You will also want to verify that the company and the agent selling you the insurance online are licensed in your state. Remember to protect your personal information online while you shop by verifying that it is a secure site (usually https:// instead of http://). If you cannot confirm that the site is secure, then consider completing the sale by mail or fax.

As always, it is best to find a trusted resource for insurance (an individual within the agent or broker organization) and keep that relationship healthy over time. Remember, when you actually need to file a claim, it is better to know a local person who is responsible for your account helping you rather than some anonymous voice or email in an impersonal customer contact center.

In Summary

Most churches today have some sort of physical location where the congregations gather for worship, study, and service. Regardless of the size and types of buildings and the campus, there will be some expense and effort required to keep the facilities safe, accessible, and beautiful.

This chapter provides a number of starting points that you can use from time to time as the need arises. However, managing building and renovation projects can be daunting. Partnering with experts outside of the church can be a needed blessing in order to make sure that the projects move to completion on time and on budget, and that they keep the larger picture in mind.

Sometimes buildings and campuses may seem to be more of a burden than a blessing. In fact, it is possible that the right response is to ultimately change locations. Prayerful discernment with your staff, advisors, and coaches/mentors will help affirm the best way of maintaining what God has provided, or it may identify what and where your church is being called to.

Chapter 8: Conclusion and Next Steps for God's Business (Your Church)

This book and its suggestions are not going to make your church successful in and of itself. As members of the Church, we need to always align our vision and focus with God's intention for us and for the world.

That being said, if we are part of an organizational structure whose purpose is to do God's work, then we owe it to God to make sure that our organizations are not only a theological and liturgical beacon to others, but also an example of an ethical and effective organizational structure that lifts up the Lord.

Those of you reading this book are either pastors or leaders who really care about your local church, and who want to make it thrive not only for the current members, but also for future generations and the community at large. In that way, you are part of a much larger community of people who are in exactly the same situation as you are. It is crucial that you connect with other pastors and leaders outside of your own circle so that you can gain insights and support from others who will not only hold you accountable, but who will support you and guide you according to their own experiences and wisdom. Being part of a network outside of your own church also allows you to be a mentor to others who can undoubtedly benefit from your experiences and love as well.

Finally, it cannot be stressed enough that you and your local church should perform an assessment of where you are currently, following the guidelines of this book. Once a thorough assessment is done, then you can identify the "low-hanging fruit" as a place to begin making the easier changes and to achieve some quick "wins", all the while looking towards bigger goals that will lead to the realization of your vision, and the advancement of the God's kingdom on Earth.

All of us who joined forces to create this book wish you and your church God's richest blessings. We pray for you, and we know that you will have a thriving ministry that transforms the lives of those whom you serve. May you be everything that God wants you to be, and if it be God's will, we hope to play some small part in your success. AMEN.

Resources

For free sample documents, useful links, and other free resources, please visit our website.

Remember to check with your denomination to find out what resources and tools they may have available for you.

Your local Chamber of Commerce may also be a good place to make connections and identify partners for existing or future projects and programs.

Bibliography

The books listed below were used to gain insights necessary for the creation of this book. Most resources are not quoted directly unless indicated in the text. I have found these books to be valuable in the understanding of good organizational processes and personal relationships.

Anthony, Michael and Estep, Jamed (ed). *Management Essentials for Christian Ministries.* B&H Publishing Group. 2005. Print.

Anthony, Scott. *The Little Black Book of Innovation: How It Works – How to Do It.* Harvard Business Review Press. 2012. Print.

Barna, George and Kinnaman, David. *Churchless: Understanding Today's Unchurched and How to Connect with Them.* Barna Group. 2014. Print.

Berger, Jonah. *Contagious: Why Things Catch On.* Simon & Schuster, 2013. Audiobook.

Christensen, Clayton. *The Innovator's Dilemma.* Harper Business. 1997. Print.

Cole, G. A. *Mangement Theory and Practice.* 6th ed. Thomson. 2004. Print.

Covey, Stephen. *The Speed of Trust: One Thing that Changes Everything.* Free Press. 2005. Print.

Hickman, Gill (ed). *Leading Organizations: Perspectives for a New Era.* 2nd ed. Sage. 2010. Print.

James, Henry. *The Ambassadors.* Rockville: Serenity, 2009. Print.

Kotter, John. *Leading Change.* Harvard Business School Press. 1996. Print.

Libby, Robert, and Libby, Patricia, and Short, Daniel. *Financial Accounting.* 7th ed. McGraw-Hill. 2011. Print.

Marshall, Greg and Johnston, Mark. *Marketing Management.* McGraw-Hill. 2010. Print.

Maxwell, John. *Leadership 101: What Every Leader Needs to Know.* Christian Audio. 2009. Audiobook.

Muehlhausen, Jim. *The 51 Fatal Business Errors and How to Avoid Them.* Maxum Communications. 2008. Print.

Rainer, Thom. *Autopsy of a Deceased Church: 12 Ways to Keep Yours Alive.* B&H Books, 2014. Print.

Packard, Josh and Hope, Ashleigh. *Church Refugees: Sociologists Reveal Why People Are Done with Church but Not Their Faith.* Josh Packard and Ashleigh Hope. 2015. Print.

Pohl, Christine. *Making Room: Recovering Hospitality as a Christian Tradition.* William Eerdmans. 1999. Print.

Seligman, Martin. *Flourish: A Visionary New Understanding of Happiness and Well-being*. Free Press. 2011. Print.

Seybold, Patricia. *Outside Innovation: How Your Customers Will Co-Design Your Company's Future*. Collins. 2006. Print.

Stetzer, Ed and Dodson, Mike. *Comeback Churches: How 300 Churches Turned Around and Yours Can Too*. B&H Publishing Group. 2007. Print.

Valacich, Joe and Schneider, Christoph. *Information Systems Today: Managing in the Digital World*. 5th ed. Prentice Hall. 2012. Print.

Wordsworth, Paul. *Lee's Building Maintenance Management*. 4th ed. Marston Book Services Ltd, 2001. Print

About the Author

When I started my first company at age 20, I desperately wanted a trusted advisor and mentor that really cared about me and what I was doing. Sadly, it was not to be, but over the years–during which I have served in the roles of CEO, employee, contractor, and a consultant (as well as preacher, teacher, small group leader, and organist/choirmaster) –I have made the invaluable discovery that the more I learn, the more I realize that I don't know.

That's where other people come in. I came to recognize that we all can succeed more quickly, and to truly flourish, by working together. We don't have to be experts on everything; we just have to be willing to give and receive help.

From this realization, LEVR Consulting (Leadership, Experience, Values, and Results), and now *God's Business*, were born. I have:

- Over 30 years of professional experience serving churches, in the industry, and across the theological spectrum.

- A proven ability to synthesize data and experience from multiple resources, allowing me to provide actionable wisdom to clients.
- An understanding on how start and grow an effective and successful organization.
- A strong clergy network across denominations and geographical boundaries.
- A commitment to sharing journeys of faith and leadership with clients, regardless of backgrounds, beliefs, and current situations.

Education credentials include:

- MBA (Master of Business Administration in Healthcare Management)
- MDiv (Master of Divinity)
- MSM (Master of Sacred Music specializing in organ performance and liturgy)
- PMP (Project Management Professional Certification).

I don't have all the answers, but together we can uncover what may be the best solution for your particular circumstance. It will be an honor to support you in its implementation and your transformation. Together We Thrive! ®

LEVR Consulting, LLC, through God's Business, seamlessly combines business and faith to create programs that provide crucial insight and practical expertise for church leaders.

Our services include:

- Mastermind Groups (online)
- One-to-one Coaching (online or in-person)
- Customized Projects for Transformation
- Church Assessment and Advisory Services
- Fundraising Projects
- Outreach and Small Group Program Development

Contact us by visiting our website:

www.gods-business.com or www.levrconsulting.com.

www.ingramcontent.com/pod-product-compliance
Lightning Source LLC
Chambersburg PA
CBHW061727020426
42331CB00006B/1134